INFORMATION MANAGEMENT

INFORMATION MANAGEMENT STRATEGIES FOR GAINING A COMPETITIVE ADVANTAGE WITH DATA

WILLIAM MCKNIGHT

Amsterdam • Boston • Heidelberg • London • New York • Oxford
Paris • San Diego • San Francisco • Sydney • Tokyo
Morgan Kaufmann is an imprint of Elsevier

Acquiring Editor: Andrea Dierna
Editorial Project Manager: Kaitlin Herbert
Project Manager: Priya Kumaraguruparan
Designer: Maria Inês Cruz

Morgan Kaufmann is an imprint of Elsevier
225 Wyman Street, Waltham, MA, 02451, USA

Library of Congress Cataloging-in-Publication Data
Application submitted

British Library Cataloguing-in-Publication Data
A catalogue record for this book is available from the British Library.

ISBN: 978-0-12-408056-0

Printed in the United States of America
14 15 16 17   10 9 8 7 6 5 4 3 2 1

For information on all MK publications
visit our website at www.mkp.com

Working together
to grow libraries in
developing countries

www.elsevier.com • www.bookaid.org

CONTENTS

FOREWORD

In 2014, it's no longer a question of *whether*[1] to become an analytics-driven organization, but *how*.

William McKnight tells us how beautifully, in this definitive book. It's an easily understood, action-oriented guide for Information Managers who want to help their organizations compete on data analytics in an era of Big Data and rapid technological innovation.

Successful analytics-driven organizations will build information architectures that match analytics workloads in the context of key questions that people in their organizations need to answer in order to create value on the front lines of their business. The best architectures will be loosely coupled so that they can absorb rapidly changing new technologies to meet competitive challenges and opportunities. Just like the one-size-fits-all database is dead,[2] the one-size-fits-all information architecture is dead.

I faced this reality personally while building out analytical informatics infrastructure as SVP and CIO at Infinity Pharmaceuticals and later as Global Head of Software and Data Engineering for Novartis Institutes for Biomedical Research (NIBR). It was also starkly clear when bringing new database and analytics products to market as a founder, advisor and investor in startups like Vertica, Data-Tamer, VoltDB and Cloudant.

This book provides an invaluable framework for making sane decisions about which technologies and approaches are right for you in building your information architecture. You'll learn how to focus your resources on solving the problems that will have the biggest impact for your business this month, quarter, and year. Competing on analytics is *not* about big multi-year projects: it's about having an impact on decision-making every day, week and month. And ensuring that when you do have a significant strategic decision to make, that you do so with the context of all the data/information available to your organization.

---

[1] Tom Davenport and Jeanne Harris made the case in their 2007 book *Competing on Analytics: The New Science of Winning*.

[2] See: http://citeseerx.ist.psu.edu/viewdoc/download?doi=10.1.1.68.9136&rep=rep1&type=pdf. One of the technologies described briefly in this paper and fully in a later paper, the C-Store column-store database, became the basis of Vertica Systems, the company that I co-founded with Michael Stonebraker in 2006.

Everyone involved in Information Management can benefit from this book: from Information Architecture experts and business-process owners to IT pros to the C-Suite. It covers the changing role of traditional analytics architecture – e.g., the data warehouse and DBMSs – and the incorporation of new analytics architecture, from column-oriented approaches and NoSQL/Hadoop to rapidly evolving IT infrastructure like cloud, open source and mobile.

Ultimately, however, this book isn't about technology or even about analytics. It's about *people* and empowering them.

Analytics starts with questions, from real people at all levels of an organization. What are the 100 (or 200 or 500) questions that would create significant value – *if* the people in your organization could answer them with the support of all the data available in your organization at any given time?

The questions that need to be answered aren't just the broad strategic questions that C-level execs talk about, but also the very tactical questions. In the past, most enterprises have focused on the former, because it cost too much and was a huge pain to extend analytics to anyone but business analysts or senior management. The technologies discussed in this book are making analytics practical for people throughout an enterprise. Democratizing analytics is a key trend that I see every day.

Great analytics provides the CONTEXT for all business people to create value throughout their day so they can make more-strategic decisions on tactical matters. Think about product support. Pretty prosaic stuff, right? Not really. When someone calls in for product support, what's the value of knowing that caller represents a top 5% customer – or whether she's even a customer? How do the support people know how to prioritize requests without analytic context?

The Information Manager's job over the next 20 years is to provide analytical context for *every* employee in the company. So that he or she can make the best decisions about how to allocate his or her time and the company's resources.

To the great information, experience and clear-thinking advice that William shares here, I'd like to add some personal observations.

- **Always start with the questions.** What are the questions that the people in your organization find most interesting and want to answer? Avoid data engineering projects that take quarters or years. Instead, embrace projects that are focused on collecting and answering *very specific* questions with high-quality data, using repeatable and sharable queries of data that interconnect sources across the company and leverage both external (publically available) and internal data.

- **Segment your workloads!** William makes a big point about this, and I totally agree. The simplest approach is by "read-oriented" and "write-oriented." Then, implement your infrastructure to ensure that there is minimal latency between your read and write systems, and you'll have something close to real time analytics. Within "read-oriented" workloads, separate read access that requires longitudinal access (a small number of records and many or all columns/fields of data) from "data mining" access (a small number of columns across many or all records). This will ensure that you can implement queries against a system designed to match the requirements of those queries – under the covers. These two types of queries are orthogonal, and the most effective way to address them is to separate these query workloads to run against systems that are designed to match the workload.

- **Remember the three key types of analytics:** descriptive, predictive and prescriptive.

Descriptive	Reporting on historical data and trends
Predictive	Reporting and exploratory on the future (which can range from very short term and tactical to very forward-looking and exploratory)
Prescriptive	Recommendations of actions based on descriptive and predictive analysis

Statistics matter for *all* analytics. But for predictive and prescriptive analytics, you can't operate without significant statistical expertise and infrastructure. R and SAS are no longer good enough. You need next-generation tools and infrastructure, most of which are not yet available in commercial third-party products. So, start with descriptive and work your way up. For an interesting reference framework for an infrastructure spanning (or ready for) all three kinds of analytics, check out Mu Sigma.[3]

- **Don't trust product vendors to optimize for you.** To minimize the number of lines of code in their systems and the cost of maintenance, product vendors usually force you into the design pattern of their product instead of setting you up with a competitive product that is better aligned with a given workload. Further, for obvious

---

[3] See http://en.wikipedia.org/wiki/Mu_Sigma_Inc.

reasons, vendors don't make it easy to integrate between products. This is one of the reasons for building a best-of-breed infrastructure (as William recommends) versus one based on a single vendor. No vendor has it all, and they are almost all radically biased towards one data engineering design pattern (row-oriented, column-oriented, document-oriented, viz-oriented, graph-oriented), Remember: one size doesn't fit all!

- **Plan for the quantity of data sources to be vast, and set up your analytics infrastructure accordingly.** Data quality matters! The best way is to control data quality at the point of data creation and by leveraging all your data sources to assess and augment any one source. Yes, the ambiguity of your data sources is significant and broad – so much so that we're going to need new ways of curating to improve and maintain data quality for *any* analytical use case. All data is valuable, but not all data is analytically relevant given the context of a specific question. This is why the collection and curation of a set of key analytical questions is so important: it helps you determine what data is analytically relevant to your organization, so you know where to invest your curation time and budget.

- **Accept that you're never done optimizing for performance.** Achieving performance requires significant effort. You'll need to integrate products from multiple vendors thoughtfully and iteratively over a long time period.

- **Push for simplicity.** Database appliances have given IT shops a taste. But I'm betting that more enterprises will realize that true simplicity comes via cloud-based solution-oriented services such as DBaaS (database-as-a-service) over the cost and complexity of maintaining dedicated physical appliances.

- **The cloud matters.** Hosted, multi-tenant databases such as such as Cloudant and Dynamo are going to be the default choice for building new systems. Eventually enterprises will realize that leveraging hosted, multi-tenant and highly optimized infrastructure is radically more cost-efficient and effective than trying to replicate the expertise required to run high-performance database systems as a service internally.

- **The future of master data management is automated data integration at scale.** This means bottom-up development of integrated models of data and meta-data using machine learning techniques – similar to the logical evolution of data virtualization.

Top-down models for information management such as "master data management" do not work. Modern analytics need more bottom-up data management and stewardship of data.

- **Focus on the real issues, not the red herrings.** Things like the NoSQL/SQL debate are just semantics, and trivialize the real struggle: *who needs access to data and how are you going to get them that data?* Most of your users don't care if you're using declarative languages such as SQL or not. Therefore, don't allow your organization to get caught up in the nonsensical narratives fueled by industry press.

Competing on analytics requires a combination of great systems and empowered, motivated people who believe in their right to information and analytics for optimal, value-creating decisions. As William emphasizes in this book, it's not either-or. It's the seamless integration of systems and people that creates non-incremental value.

We need to empower business people at the point of decision-making with analytics that will help them create significant value for their companies – every single day. *Information Management: Strategies for Gaining a Competitive Advantage with Data* is your roadmap. Good luck!

Andy Palmer

Andy Palmer is Co-Founder of Data-Tamer and Founder of Koa Labs; previously he co-founded Vertica Systems with Michael Stonebraker, PhD. A technologist and serial entrepreneur, Andy has founded, backed or advised more than 40 start-ups over the last 20 years.

IN PRAISE OF INFORMATION MANAGEMENT

"I challenge any Information Technology professional to not get value from this book. William covers a range of topics, and has so much knowledge that he is able to offer usable insights across them all. The book is unique in the way it provides such a solid grounding for anyone making architectural or process decisions in the field of information management, and should be required reading for organizations looking to understand how newer approaches and technologies can be used to enable better decision making."

– Michael Whitehead, CEO and Co-Founder, WhereScape Software

"I always enjoy William's writing, especially his balance between inspiring foresight and pragmatic advice rooted in real-world experience. He has skillfully shown that poise again: with his guidance you'll find Information Management transforms what can be a burdensome responsibility into an insightful practice."

– Donald Farmer, VP Product Management, QlikView

"Many claim we're in the golden age of data management; every traditional paradigm and approach seems to have a newer, better, and faster alternative. This book provides a terrific overview of the new class of technologies that must be integrated into every CIO's technology plan."

– Evan Levy, Co-Author of Customer Data Integration:
Reaching a Single Version of the Truth

PREFACE

Welcome to ground zero of the information age. Increasingly advanced levels of information are permeating every company, every job, every day. Companies are fine-tuning their businesses to degrees never before possible. Companies are allocating resources *selectively* to customers, products and processes. This is all a result of using information under management.

The analysis of data allows businesses to forecast market trends, consumer spending and purchasing. How we mine the data for use is an important subject that every savvy manager wants to know. Sometimes it's merely about connecting the dots that savvy managers want to know how to do.

Every time I make a purchase on Amazon, I receive suggestions of other products that I might like as well. If I make an addition purchase based on the recommendation—that's a return on investment. That's an example of the business of information.

Social networks interface with other data sources to present opportunities for consumers to sign-up for a variety of events. As consumers make selections based on choices, the information is collected for other opportunities to leverage it.

While human judgment remains vital, the nature of business judgment is changing. It must grow to utilize more information and it must utilize that information more deeply. No matter what business you are in, you are in the business of information. Most other competitive differentiators are expected in business, but it is the way a business utilizes its information today that will set it apart.

Businesses need more information, cleaner information, more well-performing information and more accessible information than their competitors to survive and thrive. And, as Chapters 10, 11 and 12 will attest, the competitive battlefield is quickly moving from traditional, alphanumeric data to "big data" and everything it brings.

All of that data needs to come from somewhere. This is not a problem as many companies are swimming in data. There is also an enormous amount of valuable external, third-party data available. If you open up to all relevant social data, fine readings of your sensor devices and all discrete movements of browsers on your websites – all the so-called "big data" – the body of data available to each company is mind-boggling. The data has to go somewhere too, and that can be challenging.

Information – the value associated with data – can be yet another story. Information should have all of the characteristics of comprehensive, clean (defined in Chapter 4), accessible and well-performing. Information is data under management that can be utilized by the company to achieve goals. Bridging that divide to solve problems you currently face is where this book comes in.

I'm a believer in the big data movement and how businesses need to capture and exploit it. Big data is just another form of data. All companies are still grappling with "non-big" (small?) data. This data has been growing too and it's vitally important for companies. This book is about turning ALL data into information.

●●●───
It's not just about "Big Data" by any stretch.
───

Starting in Chapter 2, each chapter will have a QR code at the end of the chapter which links to some additional information on the topic. In the e-book, these will be direct hyperlinks. These are links I want you to know about, and they will change over time as the subject evolves. Use your favorite QR Reader app to scan or perhaps the built-in mobile cameras of the future that will have a QR scanner.

Each chapter ends with an Action Plan, which summarizes the main take-aways of the chapter and are items to be placed in your work queue.

For Companion book site information, please visit www.informationmangementguide.com.

CHAPTER ONE

You're in the Business of Information

●●●
───

The most successful organizations are the ones with the most useful and actionable information.

───

The book is about managing bet-your-business data about customers, products, finances, suppliers, employees, vendors, etc. and all manner of transactions. The possibilities for exploiting this data have increased exponentially in the past decade. It used to be we would try to put everything in a data warehouse (discussed in the next chapter.) While those data warehouses still need attention, they're not the only game in town for data.

Technologists of all stripes in organizations are hard hit by demands for data – all data. They are also struck by the many possibilities for what to do with it.

So if this data is growing enormously, what's big and what isn't? The whole notion of what is "big" and what isn't is dealt with in Chapter 10. I believe the notion of big versus not big will go away soon. It's all data, begging to be turned into information. This book is the blueprint for corporate information.

●●●
───

Information is data taken under management that can be utilized.

───

 ## AN ARCHITECTURE FOR INFORMATION SUCCESS

The recipe for success begins with a good, well-rounded and complete architectural approach. Architecture is immensely important to information success. You can architect the environment in a way that encourages data use by making it well-performing, putting up the architecture/data quickly and having minimal impact on users and budgets for ongoing maintenance (because it was built well initially).

I have seen any or all of these factors very quickly send companies retreating to the safety of status quo information usage, instead of progressive uses of information. In the small windows most users have to engage with the data, they will reach a certain level of depth with the data. If the data is architected well, that analysis will be deep, potentially much deeper, insightful and profitable. That is the power of architecture.

This book will have case studies of architecture, but I predominately will talk about the possibilities drawing from development at dozens of companies. Every company is on the journey to information nirvana. Every step of the way in the right direction is worth it. There is no letting up.

Information Technology Disintermediation

There has been a vast disintermediation of Information Technology (IT) functions. No longer is a single IT organization in charge of everything technical. How can they be? Technology supporting information drives all aspects of the business. This makes virtually everyone part of it (lowercase IT). That's why this book is not just for those working in a formal IT organization, it's for everyone in the company pursuing their goals through technology.

Users of information are increasingly getting involved in information architecture. They are contributing to weighing the tradeoffs, assessing their workloads in deep ways, selecting methods of data movement and levels of redundancy, determining what constitutes data quality and selecting tools.

If IT is supporting an initiative – as clearly it will do for many – this book provides guideposts for that interaction. This book will provide clear guidance to formal IT as well. My point is it's information everyone in an organization needs to know. It has to do with the crown jewels, the modern-day gold of the organization – information. It's how your organization will compete.

At the same time, it also is the responsibility of those who are aware of the possibilities (through the C-suite of executives) for information in the organization to coach the organization in those possibilities and how to USE the information wisely. To whom much is given, much is required. Your capabilities grow with your wisdom about information use and management. Share the information and grow the use of information in your organization.

The Data Scientist

Are you a vaunted "data scientist" if you bring appropriate platforms under consideration or if you know how to use vast amounts of information quickly for high business gain? Yes and yes – and increasingly the answer is becoming both.

If you're waiting for the current state of affairs to get more settled, know that is unlikely to happen. Someone will champion big data. Someone will champion data virtualization (Chapter 9), data stream processing (Chapter 8) and most of the other components in this book in an organization of any size. Learn how to do it appropriately and let it be you.

Turning Information into Business Success

Today, you need to analyze your business constantly and from multiple perspectives or dimensions. There are the perspectives of the customer, the products, services, locations and many other major dimensions of the business. The high value comes from analyzing them ALL at once. You cannot simply set up a storefront, declare you are open and begin to let the business run on auto-pilot from there. You must analyze the business. Information Architecture is the key to organizing information.

THE GLUE IS ARCHITECTURE

Information must come together in a meaningful fashion or there will be unneeded redundancy, waste and opportunities missed. Every measure of optimizing the information asset goes directly to the organization's bottom line.

In reality, information management is nothing more than the continuous activity of architecture.

The glue that brings the components together is called architecture. Architecture is a high-level plan for the data stores, the applications that use the data and everything in-between. The "everything in-between" can be quite extensive as it relates to data transport, middleware and transformation. Architecture dictates the level of data redundancy, summarization and aggregation since data can be consolidated or distributed across numerous data stores optimized for parochial needs, broad-ranging needs and innumerable variations in between.

There must be a 'true north' for this enterprise information architecture and that is provided in this book. I do not provide a "one size fits all" reference architecture. Each company is going to be different. There are different starting points and different target interim ending points for architecture (it never really ends). Each company is at a different level of maturity and will wish to advance at a different pace. Many companies are not going to be able to move at the speed desired without new skills in place.

There needs to be a process in every organization to vet practices and ideas that accumulate in the industry and the enterprise and assess their applicability to the architecture. I highly advocate some company resources be allocated to "looking out and ahead" at unfulfilled, and often unspoken, information management requirements and, as importantly, at what the vendor marketplace is offering. This is a job without boundaries of budget and deadlines, yet still grounded in the reality that ultimately these factors will be in place. It's a very important job for caretaking the information management asset of an organization. For titles, I'll use Chief Information Architect.

WORKLOAD SUCCESS

Even organization leaders can take a tactical approach to the execution of the requirements. However, it does not necessarily take longer to satisfy information requirements in an architected fashion. If architecture principles and technology possibilities are not considered beforehand, the means to satisfy the current requirement may be inappropriately defaulted to the means to satisfy the last requirement. And so on.

The Chief Information Architect

The information architecture in place at any point in time is going to be a combination of a bottoms-up, needs- and workload-based approach and a top-down, longer-term thought out approach. Bottoms-up solves crises and advances tactical needs. Top-down – the job of the aforementioned Chief Information Architect among others – looks ahead. It still solves tactical issues, but does so with the strategic needs of the organization in mind. While no organization is run by either approach exclusively, can we please dial up some more top-down to avoid problems caused, essentially, by the lack of a true architecture?

The proposed approach of this book is to:

1. Have a 'true north' in mind for a 5-year information architecture, understanding that it is subject to change[1]
2. Have a Chief Information Architect managing the 5-year plan and contributing to workload architecture
3. Organize new information requirements into workloads, which comprise functionality that is necessary to achieve with data, as well as the management of the data itself
4. Allocate those workloads to the most appropriate architectural construct for its success (defined below)
5. Perform all work with an eye towards delivering return on investment (ROI) to the business at the lowest total cost of ownership (TCO)

Ultimately, we are trying to deliver return on investment to the business. It's a principle well worth following as you make decisions. ROI is [return/(return − investment)] and is always specified with a time period (i.e., 145% in 3 years). It requires the discipline of breaking down the workload into its projected cash flow. Whether you embrace the math or not, embrace the idea of delivering value to the business that could, ultimately deliver ROI. This can happen through short-term financial bottom-line impact or through information-borne innovation that yields ROI later. That is what information management should be all about − not speculation, fun exploration or a book standard. It's about business.

●●●───

By reducing fraud, a financial services provider showed a 74% 3-year ROI against the existing fraud loss trend and an insurer showed a 213% 3-year ROI through routing claims to the best provider for the service.

───

Once we have established, as a business, that a workload has high, positive ROI (relative to other possibilities for the investment), we establish the architecture for it that meets the performance, agile and scalability requirements with the lowest TCO. As such, most of this book is focused on conveying the capabilities of each platform to help you allocate workloads appropriately − with the lowest TCO! It is not designed to make you a "one percenter" in knowledge of any of the individual platforms in isolation.

---

[1] Get expert help at this. My company, McKnight Consulting Group, www.mcknightcg.com, specializes in information architecture.

Information Workloads

Allocation of workload to an architecture component is both an art and a science. There are user communities with a list of requirements upon a set of data. There are other user communities with their own list of requirements on the same data. Is this one workload? If ultimately it is best to store the data in one location and utilize the same tool(s) to satisfy the requirements, the practical answer is yes.

What Determines Workload Success

It is primarily the performance of the data access that constitutes the success of a workload[2]. Performance can be engineered (and it always must be to some degree), but primarily we give performance a huge step forward with correct workload-platform allocation.

Secondly, we need to get the workload up and running quickly. Getting to that fast performance quickly is the second measure of the success of an information workload. I talk about agile methods in Chapter 16.

Thirdly, if the good performance goes away quickly because the application is not scaling, all would be for naught. The third measure of workload success is scale. The solution should be scalable in both performance capacity and incremental data volume growth. The solution should scale in a near-linear fashion and allow for growth in data size, the number of concurrent users, and the complexity of queries. Understanding hardware and software requirements for such growth is paramount.

Note that this does not mean the initial architecture will last forever untouched. All good things come to and end and information management is no different. This does not stop us from pursuing making information as good as it can be, given what is known today.

These are the three factors I primarily consider as I give workload recommendations for the various information management platforms in this book. It does not mean there are not other factors. There are, but they tend to be "dragged along" when the focus is on these three factors. Architecture component selection is more important than ever because it must scale with exponentially increasing data volumes and user requirements.

[2] Amazon found for every 100 milliseconds of latency, they lost 1% revenue. Source: http://highscalability.com/blog/2009/7/25/latency-is-everywhere-and-it-costs-you-sales-how-to-crush-it.html

INFORMATION IN ACTION

Consider what the right architecture for an ROI-producing workload can generate for the companies below and you can see the importance of investing in wise platform selection and the need to go well beyond hanging up that storefront.

Big Box Retailer

Same store sales are dropping and the company is losing market share though web activity remains strong. It needs a way to improve its sales through understanding the dynamics of in-store and online purchasing. Through information analysis, it determines that customers who buy in-store buy much more and much more profitable items. This is partly due to impulse purchasing in the store. To boost this activity, they try to encourage online shoppers to come in to the store.

They need to make the right offer. At checkout, they encourage a store visit. For those near a store - determined using geospatial analysis - when all the products are available in the store - determined using inventory data - they extend a customized discount – approximately the cost of gas - if the buyer will come in to the store.

Also by analyzing patterns that lead to purchases and why a lot of demand is dropped shortly after a purchase pattern begins, it is determined that the main thing that causes abandonment is if the product they are interested in is not in stock. And it's not just any product in the basket – the first product into the basket counts the most, by far. By improving the information available to the shopper, the company sees more baskets go through to the sale. It also is able to better stock the most interesting items, including those in abandoned carts. If, by chance, a basket is abandoned due to an out of stock condition, they can email the shopper when the product(s) are in stock and try to recover the sale.

Telecommunications Provider

Dropped calls in a region are causing major customer defections. The company needs to know the detail about the drops - what's driving defectors and what kinds of defectors are dropping off. By creating a call graph showing who is calling who, the company gains access to the customer's value and influence circle. High value customers and influencers move immediately to a watch list.

By cross-referencing the location of dropped calls, tower coverage holes emerge. By looking at factors in the dropped calls like devices used, cell site handoffs and signal strength, causative factors might be determined.

This company can now add towers quickly to cover the high value and influential customers. They can also begin a campaign for the other high value and influential customers who will not benefit from the towers. They can issue apologies, credits, free upgrades, and possibly free cell boosters. The cell boosters cost $250 each so must be distributed judiciously. However, with the information under management, it can weigh the cost against the customer's value and likelihood to churn and can make ROI-based actions.

JUDGMENT STILL NECESSARY

I am keenly aware that, as technology expands its ever-growing footprint into all aspects of our lives, personal disruption can occur. Nowhere is technology making more strides than information management and nowhere else must personnel adapt as much as in their use of information. It is changing the nature of the company job.

Information by itself cannot think. True artificial thought – the kind that replaces human thought and judgment – should not be thought of as the next logical step in the journey. Good information management will not take the place of the skills and experience of the business analyst or data scientist. The essence of human thought is the aptitude to resolutely manipulate the meaning of the inputs encountered to create perceptibly favorable situations and arrive at a basic cognitive orientation.

It is impossible to capture all the data in empirical form that analysts utilize to make the most effective decisions. The liaison responsibilities of the analyst – between business owners, end users, IT staff and IT management – is also a necessary component of successful data analysis and operational function.

At a minimum, and where many programs are today, information management simply provides access to corporate data more efficiently and occasionally does some automated cleaning of that data. While an analyst's role in manually accumulating disparate corporate data can be diminished, the higher value-added role of thinking cannot be.

Thus, the great judgment found in the great business analysts will always be required for our success in information management. We cannot hope, nor should we strive for, any diminishment of that role with our work as information managers. It should grow, more empowered than ever before, into the new realms we'll now start to explore.

CHAPTER TWO

Relational Theory In Practice

Over 40 years ago, E. F. Codd of IBM published definitive papers on the relational database model. IBM and Oracle embraced the model early and developed commercial database systems (DBMS) that utilized the relational model.

RELATIONAL THEORY

The relational theory is quite extensive with its own set of lingo about what is eventually implemented in the DBMS[1] as a table and accessed with a form of Structured Query Language (SQL). Note that a table is not part of the relational theory, but it is the physical implementation of the relational theory—specifically the construct known as the relation. It is not necessary to fully understand the relational theory to be an expert information manager, but there is one concept about it that must be understood and that is referential integrity.

This simply means that tables are connected by keys and there can be no "orphan" records in any table. If the Customer table doesn't have customer number "123," the Order table should not record a customer number of "123." If the Product table doesn't have product code "XYZ," the Order table should not record a product code of "XYZ." This implies some ordering that is necessary for the loads and inserts into the tables. Primarily, the concept is in place to protect the tables from unwanted data. In DBMS, this function can be turned on or off.

All tables are keyed by a column or set of columns that must contain unique values.

If referential integrity is turned off, it may be for performance (referential integrity causes some overhead), in which case you would want

---

[1] We could easily put an "R" in front of DBMS to indicate relational and distinguish it from other forms of DBMS like Object DBMS (OODBMS), Network DBMS, and Hierarchical DBMS. Since I'm not recommending any of the other DBMS, or referring to them outside of this chapter, I will stick with DBMS for RDBMS.

to ensure your processes don't allow non-integrant data into the tables such as products sold that are not in the product table or trucks loaded that are not in the truck table. The function could also be turned off because processes have data loads in an order that would knowingly cause non-integrant data that will eventually become integrant. However, just allowing non-integrant data to come in without doing something about it would probably cause many problems for the system.

More detail on this is unnecessary now, but the point is that the referential integrity concept demonstrates some of the true value of the relational theory. There are numerous other concepts about which decisions must be made with any DBMS implementation. There are also numerous other DBMS objects that support the table.

The names vary from DBMS to DBMS, but I'm talking about tablespaces, databases, storage groups, indexes (explained below), synonyms, aliases, views, keys, schemas, etc. These are some of the tools of the trade for the database administrator (DBA). However, as far as the relational theory goes, it is all about the table—rows and columns.

The DBMS has been the centerpiece of information technology for 30 years. It is not going away anytime soon, either. Enterprises are absolutely bound to tables in DBMS.[2] Enterprises have anywhere from 50% to 90% of their data in tables and, if the criteria was data *under management*, it would easily be over 90% for most enterprises.

Hadoop (Chapter 11) and NoSQL databases (Chapter 10) will change this dynamic somewhat. However, the most important data in enterprises is, and will be, in DBMS. Certainly, the most important data per capita (i.e., per terabyte) in an enterprise is DBMS data.

For the data options presented in this book, here is how the DBMS is involved:

1. Data Warehouse (Chapter 6) – Implemented on DBMS
2. Cubes or Multidimensional Databases (later in this chapter) – Not exactly DBMS, but are conceptually similar
3. Data Warehouse Appliances (Chapter 6) – DBMS bundled on specialized hardware
4. Data Appliances like HANA and Exadata (Chapter 6) – DBMS bundled on specialized hardware
5. Columnar databases (Chapter 5) – DBMS with a different orientation to the data

---

[2] Most prominently, DB2, Microsoft SQL Server, Oracle, Teradata, and MySQL

6. Master Data Management (Chapter 7) – Implemented on DBMS

7. Data Stream Processing (Chapter 8) – Data layer option is not relevant as Data Stream Processing is not storing data

8. Data Virtualization (Chapter 9) – works with DBMS and non-DBMS data

9. Hadoop (Chapter 11) – Hadoop is not DBMS

10. NoSQL (Chapter 10) – NoSQL databases are not DBMS

11. Graph Databases (Chapter 12) – Graph databases are not DBMS

In addition, the operational side of a business,[3] which is not extensively covered in this book except for profound changes happening there like Master Data Management, Data Stream Processing, and NoSQL systems, is mostly run on DBMS.

It is essential to understand relational theory, as it is essential to understand how tables are implemented in DBMS. If someone were to give me an hour to describe the relational theory—the backbone of this huge percentage of enterprise data, data under management, and important data—I would quickly take the discussion to the physical implementation of the table. From this knowledge base, so much can be understood that will generate better utilized and better performing DBMS.[4] It will also help draw the comparison to NoSQL systems later.

So, let's go. This will be some of the more technical content of the book. Hang in there. Again, there absolutely is some technical material that one needs to know in order to be an excellent information manager or strategist.

The Data Page

A relational database is a file system. It's not a file system in the vernacular of how we refer to pre-DBMS file systems, but it is a *file*. It's a file that has a *repeating pattern* in the data. Most data in a DBMS is in table page or index page[5] representation and each has different patterns.

The table page's pattern repeats according to the specified size of all pages in the file, typically anywhere from 2,048 (2 k) to 32,768 (32 k) bytes. After a few overhead pages, the pages are data pages and this is what we need to focus on.

---

[3] Many of these systems are known as ERP for Enterprise Resource Planning.

[4] For a longer treatment of developing a personal knowledge base, see Chapter 5: "How to Stay Current: Technology and Skills" in my first book: McKnight, William. *90 Days to Success in Consulting*. Cengage Learning PTR, 2009.

[5] Indexes contain ordered, selective columns of the table and provide smaller, alternative structures for queries to use. They also "point" to where the "rest of the record" is in the table structure. Depending on the indexing strategy, even though indexes are subsets of the table data, all columns can be indexed and columns can be indexed multiple times.

For simplicity, I'll use 4,096 bytes (4k) as the chosen page size for the file and we'll assume that there is only one table in the file. This is not unusual.

The data page (figure 2.1) has 3 sections.[6] The first section is the page header. It is of fixed length and contains various meta information about what's going on in the page. One of the most important pieces of information is where the first free space is on the page. More on that in a moment.

Next comes the exciting part of the data page—the records. Each record has a few bytes of a record header followed by the value of every column of the table for that record. Columns are ordered in the same way for every record and every record has every column. The data manager (component of the DBMS that does the page navigation for inserts, updates, deletes, and reads) knows where every column begins because the byte count for each column is stored in the catalog.

In figure 2.1, we have customer number, company name, first name, last name, title, phone number, and email columns.

The third column of the record after an integer (4 bytes) and a 25-byte character always starts at the beginning of the record plus bytes for the record header plus 29.

This all holds true as long as the columns are fixed length. There are variable length columns where the length of the column is actually stored just in front of the column's value. The number of bytes may be 1 or 2 bytes according to the maximum length of the variable length column, but let's say it is 2 bytes. That's 2 bytes stored for the column plus, of course, the actual value, itself.

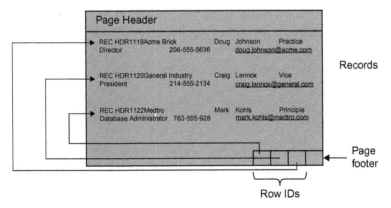

Figure 2.1 Relational Data Page Layout.

---

[6] In addition to a small "page footer" which acts like a check digit.

The data manager will have to read those length bytes to know where all columns *following* this column *start*. This presents some additional overhead, which is why a rule of thumb is to store the variable length columns at the *end* of the record.[7]

Columns that may be null (no value) will have a byte[8] prepended to the value that will have 2 values possible—one representing the column is null (in which case, the value is ignored), the other representing that the column is not null (in which case, the value is good and will be read). The data manager will, naturally, understand this additional byte is part of the column length and use it when calculating offsets to column starts.[9]

Finally, a hugely important aspect of the DBMS is the row identifiers or row IDs (RIDs). These are bytes (the number of which is dependent on page size, but I'll use 2 bytes per row ID) that start from the *end* of the page and are allocated *backwards* within the page as records are added to the page. There is one row ID per record on the page and it contains the offset from the beginning of the page to where that record (record header) begins. The number of row IDs equals the number of records on the page.

●●●
_____

The offset from the beginning of the file to the beginning of a data page is going to be the sum of:
- The number of "overhead" pages at the beginning of the file, typically 1–3, times the page size
- The page number minus one times the page size

For example, to get to the 100th page of a table where the page size is 4k and there are 2 overhead pages, the data manager will start at the beginning of the file and advance:
- 4k times 2 for the overhead pages
- 4k times 99 to get to the start of the 100th page

_____

The number of records a page can hold primarily depends on the size of the record versus the size of the page. If the records are really small, however, the number of row IDs could actually be exhausted before the space is fully utilized. In figure 2.1, we see that there are 3 records on this page.

In general, DBAs have been increasing page sizes for analytic workloads over the years. Some shops understand why and other shops do not. The primary reason is that the bottleneck is I/O and we need our DBMS to, when it finally gets to the point of doing an I/O, grab as much information as

---

[7] Although some DBMS group the VARCHARs at the end of the record automatically.

[8] A bit would do, but everything is done on a byte boundary.

[9] Some DBMS group multiple null bytes into one byte.

is reasonably possible at that point. Since the page is the usual unit of I/O, this means the page sizes are getting bigger. I'll have more on this in Chapter 5 on columnar databases, where I talk about how they tackle this problem.

NewSQL

Products in the NewSQL category are an implementation of relational SQL in scale out (described in Chapter 10); in-memory (described in Chapter 6) architectures, which provide relational database functions for high performance, high throughput transactional workloads, such as storing capital market data feeds, placing financial trades, absorbing entire record streams in telecommunications, supporting online gaming, and supporting digital exchanges.

A newly allocated table's data pages will have no records and the first usable space is just after the page header. Once records begin to fill on the page, the usable space begins to shrink and the starting point for the next record advances. The page header contains where this starting point is to help the data manager place records. Simple enough, but what about when a record is deleted?

Deletions create "holes" on the page. The data page changes very little physically except noting the record is invalid. Holes get chained together on the page. If a record has turned into a hole, there is a pointer to the next hole in the record header. If the data manager wants to use this page to place a record to, for example, force ordering of data in the table (as in the use of a "clustering" index), it will do a "mini-reorg" of the page to collapse the holes and create more available space. You see, it is the order of the records in the row IDs that count (in terms of the records being "in order"), not the physical ordering of the records on the page.

If you are forcing a customer number ordering on the table, the customer numbers could get jumbled *on* the page, but the row IDs will surely be pointing to records with increasing customer numbers.

These DBMS are extremely math-driven. By doing microsecond calculations, the DBMS gets the I/O where it needs to get to retrieve the record. It's off the disk as binary, translated to hexadecimal, and on to the ASCII that we appreciate! This is, in a nutshell, how the data page works. The other large chunk of DBMS space is for indexes.

Indexes

Indexes take single or multiple columns out of a table into a different physical structure, where the values are kept in order regardless of the ordering of the table. This is a structure where "random access" is possible because of the ordering. There are also structure pages (called "nonleaf") that help guide the DBMS in understanding on what index pages certain values are. The DBMS will traverse these structure pages to get to the "leaf" pages, which is where the index entries are.

Index entries are comprised of the key plus the RID(s)[10] for where the "rest of the record" is in the table. For example, if there were an index on company name, an entry might be:

ACME BRICK | 100-1

This means the company name of "ACME BRICK" can be found on page 100, row ID 1. For SELECT * WHERE COMPANYNAME = "ACME BRICK", it would be much more efficient to look this up quickly in the index and then go to page 100 in the table to get the other fields for the result set (as opposed to reading every table entry to see if it's for ACME BRICK).

That's the beauty of the index. There are many kinds of indexes and the navigation patterns differ according to kind, but they are mostly for one purpose—performance.[11] The DBMS's optimizer works with the index structures to determine the most appropriate "path" to take within the data to accomplish what is necessary.

Optimizers are pretty smart. Most use an estimated cost basis approach and will forge the lowest cost path for the query. While all these machinations can seem to work fine "behind the scenes," DBMSs benefit tremendously from excellent database administrators (DBAs). Without some knowledge of their work or points of communication, enterprises are hostages to their DBAs, as well as undervaluing them.

MULTIDIMENSIONAL DATABASES

Multidimensional databases (MDBs), or cubes, are specialized structures that support very fast access to summarized data. The information data store associated with multidimensional access is often overshadowed by the robust data access speed and financial calculation capabilities. However, as additional structures that need to be maintained, the multidimensional databases create storage and processing overhead for the organization.

---

[10] Why the "(s)"? Because, in nonunique indexes (most indexes are nonunique), multiple records can have the same value for the key (e.g., multiple records for ACME BRICK company name).

[11] Although some index types also force table order or uniqueness among the values.

The data access paradigm is simple:
1. What do you want to see?
2. What do you want to see it *by*?
3. What parameters do you want to put on the dimensions?
   For example:
1. I want to see sales
2. I want to see sales by state
3. I want to limit the result set to the Southwest region (from the geographic dimension)

Cube access is referred to as online analytical processing (OLAP) access. Specifically, the cube implements the multidimensional form of OLAP access, or MOLAP access. ROLAP, for relational OLAP, refers to the utilization of the data access paradigm upon a relational (not a cube) structure. ROLAP is just glorified SQL. Since I'm advocating the primary continuance of a ton of DBMS and SQL in the enterprise, I'll just lump ROLAP into SQL use. ROLAP is not a platform like MOLAP is.

Back to multidimensional databases, they are what I call "hyperdimensional." The logical model is dimensional, but the physical rendering is fully denormalized so there are no "joins." Like a data warehouse, they are built from source data. The point that must be made is that these structures grow (and build times grow) tremendously with every column added. The data access layer hides the complex underlying multidimensional structure.

This structure includes all the columns of the source tables physically "pre-joined," such that there are no joins in the data access. The rows are then compressed and indexed within the MDB so it is able to do random access.

If a query is paired well with the MDB (i.e., query asks for the columns of the MDB—no more and no less), the MDB will outperform the relational database, potentially by an order of magnitude. This is the promise that many reach for in MDBs. However, most of the time growing cubes and, therefore, growing the load cycle and the storage, is far too tempting. The temptation to think that because some queries perform well, the MDB will be adopted for all queries, can be too much to resist. One client of mine began rebuilding "the cube" on Fridays at 5:00 pm and half of the time, it was not complete by Monday at 9:00 am.

●●●—————————————————————————————

Beware of multidimensional hell.

Multidimensional databases (MDB) are a "last resort" when a highly tuned relational database will not give the performance that is required. MDBs can be quickly built to support a single query or just a few queries, but there often is a high price for this approach.

Since many multidimensional databases land in companies as a result of coming in with packaged software, it must also be said that if the overall package provides a true return on investment—versus the alternative of building the package functionality in the shop—then that is another valid reason for a multidimensional database.

If you do have MDBs, ensure that the maintenance (cycles, storage) is well understood. MDBs can support workloads that are well-defined and understood. Otherwise, tread lightly.

RDBMS PLATFORMS

A DBMS, technically, is software and not a platform. I'll talk here about some various hardware that the DBMS might reside upon. Together, DBMS and hardware make a platform for data. In this chapter, I will avoid the pre-bundled data warehouse appliance and data appliance and stick with advisement for the many cases where the DBMS and hardware are separate and you, or your vendor, are putting DBMS onto hardware, like Legos, to create your platform.

Most major DBMSs are a far cry from the early days. They have innovated along with the demand. They have grown in their capabilities and continue to grow. They have not, however, obviated, in any way, the need for appliances, stream processing, master data management, or the growing NoSQL movement. Chapters 10–12 will talk about their workloads. The information management pot has only swelled with these advances.

One of the major areas of focus is not in DBMS features, but in where the DBMS stores its data.

The decision point is the allocation and juxtaposition of storage across hard disk drives (HDD) and flash-based solid state drives (SSD), the accompanying allocation of memory, and the associated partitioning strategy (hot/cold)[12] within the data. Throw in the compression strategy, also key to a successful DBMS architecture, and—as long as cost matters (per capita costs are falling, but data is growing)—you have a complex architecture that cannot be perfect.

---

[12] data temperature.

The issue of HDD v. SSD v. Memory comes down to cost versus performance: dollars per GB v. pennies per GB for vastly different read rate performance. The cost of more than 40% to SSD or Memory is prohibitive to most workloads. However, there are many other factors to consider as well, including durability, start-up performance, write performance, CPU utilization, sound, heat, and encryption.

Teradata machines, for example, automatically determine what is hot and cold and allocate data based on usage. As Dan Graham, General Manager Enterprise Systems at Teradata, put it: "DBAs can't keep up with the random thoughts of users" so hard or fixed "allocating" data to hot/cold is not a good approach. Get a system that learns and allocates. Business "dimensional" data—like customers, products, stores, etc.—tend to be very hot and therefore stay in the hot option, but, again, this is based on actual usage.

All of this doesn't help to determine how much and what percentage of overall space to make HDD, SSD, and Memory. On an average system, it ends up being between 50 and 70 percent HDD. It's based on workload (if migrating) or anticipated workload (for new systems) and an attempt to get "most" of the I/Os on SSD and Memory.

Memory is certainly a huge factor in allocating budget to need. A strong memory component can mitigate the value of SSD when it comes to reads, but may produce inconsistent response times. Transactional databases will move to more memory-based solutions faster than analytical workloads due to the variability of performance with memory.

In-memory capabilities will be the corporate standard for the future, especially for traditional databases, where disk I/O is the bottleneck. In-memory based systems do not have disk I/O. Access to databases in main memory is up to 10,000 times faster than access from storage drives. Near-future blade servers will have up to 500 gigabytes of RAM. Already, systems are being sold with up to 50 terabytes of main memory. Compression techniques can make this effectively 10x–20x that size in data.

SAP BusinessObjects introduced in-memory databases in 2006 and is the first major vendor to deliver in-memory technology for BI applications. There are currently many database systems that primarily rely on main memory for computer data storage[13] and few that would claim to be absent any in-memory capabilities or a roadmap with near-term strong in-memory capabilities.

Also, many architectures have flash memory on their SSD. Apples-to-apples comparisons are hard to come by, but there is experience, knowledge and references that serve as guideposts. Every

---

[13] or solely rely on memory for the storage, such as HANA from SAP.

situation is different. Please call us at (214) 514–1444 if you want to discuss yours.

> ### Use of Solid State Drives
> A few systems that very effectively utilize SSD are part of this growing movement and are likely to have their descendants relevant for a long time, including: Fusion-io, IBM's XIV, and Violin Memory.

Fusion-io

Fusion-io is a computer hardware and software systems company based in Cottonwood Heights, Utah, that designs and manufactures what it calls a new memory tier based on NAND Flash memory technology. Its chief scientist is Steve Wozniak. Fusion-io technology primarily sells through partnerships.

IBM's project Quicksilver, based on Fusion-io technology, showed that solid-state technology in 2008 could deliver the fastest performance of its time: 1 million Input/Output Operations Per Second.

IBM XIV

IBM XIV Storage System Gen3's SSD caching option is being designed to provide up to terabytes of fast read cache to support up to a 90% reduction in I/O latency for random read workloads.

Violin Memory

Violin Memory is based in Mountain View, California, and designs and manufactures enterprise flash memory arrays that combine Toshiba NAND flash, DRAM, distributed processing, and software to create solutions like network–attached storage (NAS), local clusters, and QFabric data centers from Juniper Networks.

It's DRAM-based rack-mounted SSD.

Violin was refounded and recapitalized by Don Basile, ex–CEO of Fusion-io. He brought a few members of his previous team, and Violin Memory is now considered the leading flash memory array vendor in the industry.

Current configurations are either 16 Terabytes of SLC flash or 32 Terabytes of MLC.

Keep an eye on the QR Code for developments in DBMS use of SSD and memory-based systems.

ACTION PLAN

1. Inventory your use of relational databases to see how prominent they are in the environment
2. Inventory your collective knowledge of relational databases to understand if you have the skills to optimize this important data store
3. Inventory your multidimensional databases and reduce your overcommitment to this platform
4. Stop any mindset that favors MDBs as the default way to access enterprise data
5. Move your most important, real-time requirements to a DMBS with a strong in-memory component
6. Only procure new DBMS platforms that well utilize SSD
7. Deploy DBMS with 20%–40% SSD
8. Consider NewSQL to replace underperforming relational transactional systems and for new transactional systems with high performance and high throughput requirements

CHAPTER THREE

You're in the Business of Analytics

I am now going to present a caveat to the premise of Chapter 1—that you are in the business of information. While undoubtedly that is true, it is a *form* of information that is prominent enough to replace information in the mantra, and that form is analytics.

Basic information operates the business and it is available in abundance to accumulate, publish, and be available from the myriad of data stores I will discuss in this book. Basic information provides rearview-mirror reporting and some nearsighted ability to look forward and get ahead the next few feet.

When it comes to seeing the business landscape to make process change or to strive for maximum profitability derived from customer- and product-specific catering, you need forward-facing data. You need to know a future that you can intervene in and change. You need to know the future that will not actually happen because you're intervening and turning it in a more profitable direction.

The lack of precise forecasting, caused by constant change, may leave the analytics process in doubt. Yet, you must build up trust in the analytic process through trust in the quality data, the right models, and the application of those models in the business.

WHAT DISTINGUISHES ANALYTICS?

Many approach analytics as a set of value propositions to the company. However, from a data use perspective, the definition of analytic data relates to how it is formed. It is formed from more complex uses of information than reporting. Analytic data is formed from summarized data providing information that is used in an analytic process and yielding insightful information to be used in decision making.

Addressing the propensity of a customer to make a purchase, for example, requires an in-depth look at the spending profile—perhaps by time slice, geography, and other dimensions. It requires a look at those with similar demographics and how they responded. It requires a look at ad effectiveness. And it may require a recursive look at all of these and more. Analytics should also be tied to business action. A business should have actions to take as a result of analytics—for example, customer-touch or customer-reach programs.

There are numerous categories that fit this perspective of analytics. Customer profiling, even for B2B customers, is an essential starting point for analytics.

Companies need to understand their "whales" (most valued customers) and how much they are worth comparatively. Companies need a sense of the stages or states a customer goes through with them and the impact on revenue when a customer changes stages. Customer profiling sets up companies for greatly improved targeted marketing and deeper customer analytics.

This form of analytics starts by segmenting the customer base according to personal preferences, usage behavior, customer stage, characteristics, and economic value to the enterprise. Economic value typically includes last quarter, last year-to-date, lifetime-to-date, and projected lifetime values.

Profit is the best metric in the long run to use in the calculations. However, spend (shown in the bullets below) will work, too. More simple calculations that are simply "uses," like purchases, of the company's product will provide far less reliable results.

The key metrics to use should have financial linkage that maps directly to the return on investment (ROI) of the company. Where possible, analyze customer history for the following econometric attributes at a minimum:

- Lifetime spend and percentile rank to date (This is a high-priority item.)
- Last year spend and percentile rank (This is a high-priority item.)
- Last year-to-date spend and percentile rank
- Last quarter spend and percentile rank
- Annual spend pattern by market season and percentile rank
- Frequency of purchase patterns across product categories
- Using commercial demographics (Polk, Mediamark or equivalent), match the customers to characteristic demographics at the block group[1] levels
- If applicable, social rank within the customer community
- If applicable, social group(s) within the customer community

---

[1] Subset of a city; a geographic unit used by the United States Census Bureau.

These calculations provide the basis for customer lifetime value and assorted customer ranking. The next step is to determine the attributes for projected *future* spend. This is done by assigning customers a lifetime spend. Lifetime spend is based on (a) n-year performance linear regression or (b) n-year performance of their assigned quartile,[2] if less than n years of history is available.

> ## Customer Lifetime Value: The Prima Facie Analytic
> CLV = Present Value (future profits (revenues minus expenses) from customer in *n* years)
>
> There are three major components to the formula: revenues, length of the relationship (n), and expenses.
>
> Revenues. Future revenues are largely based on recent past revenues. With a few years of data and more sophistication, regression of past revenue forward serves to determine future revenues.
>
> Length of the Relationship. Retention modeling can be used to understand leading indicators for customer drop off. Calculating CLV for different estimated customer lifetimes shows the value of keeping the customer for longer periods; this shows the potential CLV. Most organizations that do this valuable exercise are amazed at the potential CLV of their customers and how it grows over time.
>
> The goal becomes keeping the customers with highest CLV as long as possible and reverse engineering the attributes of those high CLV customers for use with marketing behavior, thereby increasing overall CLV. Retention modeling usually accompanies CLV modeling.
>
> Expenses. The major difficulty in computing CLVs is not in computing customer income. It's on the expense side of the ledger. It can be difficult to determine how to allocate company expenses to a particular customer, but it's immensely worthwhile.

Choose key characteristics of each customer quartile, determine unique characteristics of each quartile (age, geography, initial usage), match new customers to their quartile and assign average projected spend of that quartile to new customers.

Defining the relevant and various levels of retention and value is an extension of customer profiling. These are customer profiling variables like the ones above except they are addressing the need for more immediate preventative action as opposed to predicting the volume of future profit.

---

[2] A quartile is 25% of the customer base. You could do more divisions (quintile) or fewer (decile). The point is a few, manageable profiles.

Also, regardless of churn[3] potential, the determination of the point at which customers tend to cross a customer stage in a negative direction is essential to analytics.

Customer profiling and customer stage modeling should combine to determine the who and when of customer interaction. Actions are dependent on the company but could be a personal note, free minutes, free ad-free time, and/or free community points.

In addition, in markets where customers are likely to utilize multiple providers for the services a company provides, the company should know the aspirant level of each customer by determining the 90th percentile of usage for the customers who share key characteristics of the customer (age band, geography, demographics, initial usage). This "gap" is an additional analytic attribute and should be utilized in customer actions.

This is simply a start on analytics, and I've focused only on the customer dimension, but hopefully it is evident that many factors make true analytics:

- Analytics are formed from summaries of information
- Inclusion of complete, and often large, customer bases
- Continual recalculation of the metrics
- Continual reevaluation of the calculation methods
- Continual reevaluation of the resulting business actions, including automated actions
- Adding big data to the mix extends the list of attributes and usability of analytics by a good margin

Big Data and Analytics

With the ability to explore previously unrealized correlations between certain metrics and/or attributes, big data—and the combination of big data and relational data—greatly increases the effectiveness of analytics. While big data enhances analytics with additional, albeit very granular, data points, it also opens up the possibilities for analytics, taking them into the realm of minute fine-tuning.

If we're in the business of analytics and analytics are required, it stands to reason that eventually it's analytics comprising *all* data, especially the mammoth big data, that will create the leading businesses of tomorrow.

---

[3] When a customer becomes a *former* customer through an act of attrition or inactivity, as determined by the company.

Consider the field of telematics (i.e., automobile systems that combine global positioning satellite (GPS) tracking and other wireless communications for various purposes: automatic roadside assistance, remote diagnostics, etc.), which has serious traction in the auto insurance industry, most famously by Progressive Insurance. If a consumer opts in by placing a sensor device in their car, which feeds its data to the insurance company, they can save money on their insurance. These devices capture fine movements of the car and the car's location, both of which decrease the odds to very minimal that the insurance package would be less than profitable.

Many using big data analytics to personalize products for customers—such as Netflix, which can recommend movies that model a selection pattern and Amazon, which offers customized recommendations for purchases based on buying habits. Another example is an electric company that offers personalized energy management alerts and recommendations based on smart meters, enabling customers to be in the appropriate plan for them.

Health insurance companies routinely analyze customer health records, correlating granular statistics about patient conditions to outcomes. Green energy systems can increase output with minute adjustments to energy conversion devices like wind turbines. Social media is mined for customer preferences and best times, locations and wording for posting to social networking services. And, of course, for better or worse, governments monitor citizen activity by tracking communications and movements. Most video, phone, and internet activity, with many pixels, sound waves, and fine cursor movement being recorded in subseconds, is big data.

PREDICTIVE ANALYTICS

Analytics is a business strategy that must be supported with high quality, cross–platform–border data, as just discussed. The data is formed in order to make predictions about the business. We use "*Predictive* Analytics" to refer to the class of analytics focused on creating a better future for the company, from grand process change to individual customer interactions.

If done well, predictive analytics help companies avoid business situations analogous to being struck by a bus. Business situations, however, are usually less dramatic and much more nuanced than avoiding a moving vehicle. And, unlike the bus, a company will often not even know there was a situation worth avoiding.

Therein lies the fate of many analytics—in order to prove its worth, you need to build trust in your predictions. Occasionally, I have let predictions of minor doom pass with a client in order to build trust ("We had 142 churners in Maine this month, just like the model predicted. Now can we apply the model nationwide and *prevent* the churn?").

Predictive analytics are key to the prevention of loss by fraud, churn and other unwanted outcomes—the equivalents of being hit by the bus.

The Analytics Approach

1. Control data systemically that is detailed, accessible, wide-ranging, and well-performing
2. Focus on a business problem
3. Choose a modeling technique
4. Build models to translate the data into probable business actions, with associated probability of action
5. Avoid the undesired future with effective business action
6. Evaluate effectiveness
7. Refine the model
8. Repeat

Predictions should be communicated as a probability distribution. This turns model output such as "likely to be fraudulent" into "75% likely to be fraudulent." This can better correspond to a range of actions appropriate to the event (fraud) *and* the percentage (75%).

In terms of "avoiding the undesired future with effective business action," these are the next steps that turn all of the data analysis and preparation and the building of the model into business.

BUILDING PREDICTIVE ANALYTIC MODELS

Predictive analytics are applied in the process of determining business events that are likely to occur and be actionable. The probability threshold of "likely" differs from event to event.

Companies that do predictive analytics without attaching a probability to events are seriously impeding the profit potential of predictive analytics.

Company profiles also come into play. Actions take cycles and a fast-moving company driving a strong top line is going to care about something different than an established multinational company with

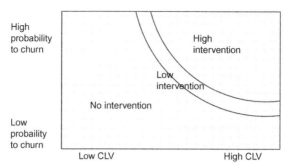

Figure 3.1 Decision model with churn management.

a large customer base and low margins. The former may only prepare for relatively low probability events that come with a particularly bad outcome or try to only enact change that leads to high increased profitability. The latter companies are more risk averse and will seize every opportunity to move the needle even slightly.

A predictive modeler might produce a result that indicates a customer is likely to churn, yet the model might not indicate how likely it is to happen or whether the company should care about this.

There is a set of company reactions to any likely unwanted business event or business opportunity. These range from highly invasive actions, like terminating the credit card, to simply changing a metric about the customer that may, one day, lead to a more invasive action if compounded. And, of course, there's "do nothing."

Example 1 Customer Lifetime Value

Customer lifetime value is a means to an end. It supports operations as a data point to justify taking other actions, such as whether to market to a person/company, how to support the customer, whether to approve financing, whether to challenge a transaction as fraudulent, etc.

Example 2 Churn Management

When a customer appears likely to churn, companies are increasingly turning to customer lifetime value and other predictive analytics to temper the instinct to rush to salvage the relationship. The operative term is "churn management," not "churn prevention."

Regardless, proactive intervention to salvage the relationship, if so desired, is a multidimensional decision.

Example 3 Clinical Treatment

Caregiving organizations want to provide the best care at the lowest cost. To reach this balance, multiple procedures for the patient are considered based on probabilities of efficacy. This efficacy is formed from transaction patterns and, increasingly, big data read from monitoring.

Example 4 Fraud Detection

Predictive analytics is used to determine the potential fraudulent nature of a transaction. Here again, we find that analyzing a transaction without bringing to bear a customer profile built on summarized and recent transactions can lead to false assumptions and actions. Increasingly, a customer profile is required input for any model performing fraud detection.

But on a larger and broader scale, another trend is bringing more data into the predictions, and that includes web-scale data and other big-data environments. For example, customer usage burdens on support can contribute to expenses in the CLV calculation.

Example 5 Next Best Offer

Descriptive modeling classifies customers into segments that are utilized in a large variety of marketing-related activities. These segments should be formed dynamically in conjunction with campaigns and should correlate to the various activities of the campaign. Rather than marketing to everyone determined "likely to purchase," a "probability to purchase" should be produced and used with other factors that make the effort worthwhile to the company in the long run. A factor like the customer's income might increase the company's interest in encouraging the customer through a smartphone or tablet app alert.

A related use of predictive analytics is in decision modeling, which might focus on the next customer interaction and whether it should be proactive and driven by the company (like extending an offer) or reactive (like responding to a financing application).

Proving the need for multiple dimensions in predictive analytics is like proving I should not have stepped in front of that bus. It's sometimes hard to demonstrate what you have prevented.

ANALYTICS AND INFORMATION ARCHITECTURE

You are going to learn quite a bit in this book about the various types of data stores that are legitimate for corporate data. As you travel through the data stores, you may wonder where to place your analytic data and where to actually do the analytic processing. Analytic data is increasingly interesting everywhere processing is done. It will be important to make the analytic data accessible to every data store if the data is not actually *in* the data store.

In the chapter on master data management, I will make a case for Master Data Management (MDM) to be a primary distribution point, perhaps in addition to being the system that originates some of the analytic data.

As far as analytic processing goes, the goals of all the processing that goes on throughout the enterprise is only enhanced with analytic data. Many enterprises already acknowledge that they "compete on analytics." Many more will join them.

Analytics are used to assess current markets and new markets to enter. They are used in determining how to treat customers and prospects, in very detailed ways. They are used for bundling and pricing products and services and marketing products and services. And clearly they are used to protect a company's downside, like fraud, theft, and claims.

You may have a workable supply chain that gets a product to the store (or whatever passes for a store in your business), have low prices, and tactically everything may seem to "work." That is not enough today. Today, the supply chain must be very efficient, prices should be set based on a firm grounding in analysis, and customers must be known at an intimate level.

The use of analytics comprises the major area of competitive focus for organizations in the foreseeable future.

ANALYTICS REQUIRES ANALYSTS

A host of articles and books have promoted the idea that nearly full company automation is possible, supported by analytics, which are also automated. This automation rivals the intellectual properties of the business analyst who currently translates these analytics into the achievement of company goals. These systems will purportedly exhibit behaviors that could be called intelligent behavior.

The question is not whether or not information systems supported by analytics reason. Of course, they will not. Nor is the question whether or not systems will be able to create the illusory effect of reasoning. They will also clearly get better at it. Information management displays apparently intelligent behavior when it automatically alters in-process promotions to be rerouted to prospect profiles that are responding to the initial mailing. When information management uses analytics to reroute procedures to best-of-breed providers, it displays intelligence. Additionally, when it uses analytics to automatically change pricing in response to demand, it displays intelligence.

However, good engineering cannot yet take the place of the skills and experience of the business analyst. The essence of human reason is the aptitude to resolutely manipulate the meaning of the inputs encountered to create perceptibly favorable situations and arrive at a basic cognitive orientation. The development of this ability within the experienced business analyst makes him or her more adaptable to the business environment. This is what business analysts do—they reason. Analytics don't.

Determination of the best fit of data for broad organizational needs is another multidimensional reasoning function many business analysts provide to an organization. Business and data requirements are seldom able to be completely coded. Requirements misfire frequently.

At a minimum, and where many programs are today, business intelligence simply provides access to corporate data more efficiently and occasionally does some automated cleaning of that data. While an analyst's role in manually accumulating disparate corporate data can be diminished with good information management, the higher value-added role of reasoning cannot be. There are, clearly, non-analytical, operational functions being served up to automation, such as industrial manufacturing.

Computers are better at fast calculations than analysts, but that's not reasoning. There is no scalability from syntactical computation to the input manipulation, abstraction, and perception—the functions that comprise reasoning—based on continued innovation in information management and advances in computational power alone.

The chances of successful analytics efforts significantly correlate with having people with the right characteristics for success on the project. This success goes far beyond technical skills. Analytics work best when they foster organizational communication.

Putting together the data, the processes, *and the people* around analytics has created the most successful businesses in the world. Welcome to the business of analytics.

ACTION PLAN

- Survey your use of information—are your users using only base information or is it pre-summarized and enhanced to draw real, actionable meaning out of it prior to user interface
- Ensure analytics are a part of corporate strategy
- Enlist the support of business representation in determining the analytic calculations and predictive models
- Determine the analytic data that will be useful to your business strategy
  - Understand the calculations on base information necessary to bring the data to full utility
  - Understand where the base information resides today and if it is in a leverageable place

CHAPTER FOUR

Data Quality: Passing the Standard

Before we get too far into the platforms that will store the information and analytics our companies need, I need to issue a warning. Data anywhere in the enterprise ecosystem that is considered of poor quality will be detrimental to the information manager's goals, to any system affected, and to overall company goals. Though there is a lot of work involved in the platform itself, focusing strictly on the platform and ignoring the quality of the data that goes in it will be done at great peril.

How many applications could successfully maximize their function with "dirty data" stemming from poorly designed data models? Could cross-selling and upselling be maximized if the customers were not unique and their data was not complete or the products were at different levels of granularity or had incorrect attribution? Could you do credit card fraud detection or churn management correctly if you did not have the customer's transaction pattern correct? Many of these applications have failed in the past because they were not supported with sufficiently clean, consistent data of the business entities such as common definitions of customer, prospect, product, location, part, etc.

It is important to understand the flow of information in the business ecosystem and to inject data quality into the ecosystem at the most leverageable points—those systems that serve the function of data distribution. The master data management hub, as well as other systems of origination, are some of the most leverageable components and should epitomize data quality. The data warehouse is leverageble to the post-operational analytics environment. In reality, each environment (even big data ones) needs data to be up to a standard prior to its use.

Data quality should be suitable to a particular purpose, and that purpose changes from operational systems to Master Data Management (MDM) to data warehouse. For example, classification data is often neglected in operational systems because it doesn't impact effective transaction processing. It's addressed more effectively in MDM solutions in which classification data is more of a focus, such as identification data in MDM and data warehouse solutions that integrate such data from multiple domains of values (e.g., stock ticker and CUSIP as two separate domains of identification values for the same entities). A key concept here is suitability to purpose.

That is the mentality for how I'll define data quality—data that is void of intolerable defects. These intolerable defects should be defined according to the uses of the data. There is no national, industry, or vendor standard that you should aspire to. Data quality takes effort. It must be time (and money) well spent. Chasing what someone else decided is good for the system is not the best use of time—unless that someone else is the data steward.

> ### Data Quality Defined
> Data quality is the absence of intolerable defects. It is not the absence of defects. Every enterprise will have those. It is the absence of defects that see us falling short of a standard in a way that would have real, measurable negative business impact. Those negative effects could see us mistreating customers, stocking shelves erroneously, creating foolish marketing campaigns, or missing chances for expansion. Proper data quality management is also a value proposition that will ultimately fall short of perfection, yet will provide more value than it costs.
>
> The proper investment in data quality is based on a bell curve on which the enterprise seeks to achieve the optimal ROI at the top of the curve. Here is a simple example: an e-commerce/direct mail catalog/brick-and-mortar enterprise (e.g., Victoria's Secret), regularly interacts with its customers. For e-commerce sales, address information is updated with every order. Brick-and-mortar sales may or may not capture the latest consumer address, and direct mail catalog orders will capture the latest address.
>
> However, if I place an order and move two weeks later, my data is out-of-date: short of perfection. Perfection is achievable, but not economically achievable. For instance, an enterprise could hire agents in the field to knock on their customers' doors and monitor the license plates of cars coming and going to ensure that they know to the day when a customer moves. This would come closer to perfect data on the current address of consumers, but at tremendous cost (not to mention that it would irritate the customer). The point: the data needs to provide more value than it costs.

The data steward represents the business interest in the data and will articulate the rules and provide most of the manual changes necessary to data. The sidebar further describes the roles of the data steward in information management. Please note this is not an abdication of overall data quality responsibility or an excuse for the information manager to not lead or bring ideas to the table. The bottom line responsibility for data quality lies with the information manager.

> ### Data Stewardship Roles and Responsibilities
> Data stewards should come from business areas, be assigned on a subject-area basis and perform the following roles for information in the enterprise.
> 1. Determining the data sources
> 2. Arbitrating the transformation rules for data
> 3. Verifying the data
> 4. Contributing the business description of the data[1]
> 5. Supporting the data user community
> 6. Contributing to the overall information management program governance
> 7. Ensuring data quality
>
> [1] The "business metadata"

Since every organization will already have information management components in place, it may be necessary to prioritize remediation efforts. Many times the systems needing improved data quality are obvious. Other times, it requires some profiling. Profiling should be done as a check against the current state of the data in relation to potential defects. It's a hunt for specific data quality violations, not a general hunt for general data flaws.

DATA QUALITY DEFECT CATEGORIES

So, together with the data steward(s) and with an understanding of how the data will be used (both directly and downstream), here are the categories of data quality rule violations:

- Referential Integrity
- Uniqueness
- Cardinality
- Subtype/Supertype
- Reasonable Domains
- Multiple Meaning Columns
- Formatting Errors
- Optional Data
- Derived Data
- Complete Data
- Incorrect Data
- Data Codification

Referential Integrity

Referential integrity (RI) refers to the integrity of reference between data in related tables. For example, product identifiers in sales records need to also be found in the product tables. RI is essential in preventing users from navigating to a "dead end." Many transactional systems utilize database-enforced RI, but many other systems like data warehouses[2] do not, due to the performance and order restrictions it places on data loading. But RI is still important and must be enforced somehow. In the target marketing system, for example, incorrect RI may mean sales with an undefined product and/or to an undefined customer, which effectively takes that sale out of the analysis.

Uniqueness

Column(s) assigned to uniquely identify a business entity, like a product identifier, should also be unique. It constitutes a violation when the same identifier is used to identify multiple products. This also has implications for RI. Not only do we not want dead-end navigations in the data, but we also do want a singular reference. In the target marketing system, for example, a single product for product identifier 123 is expected.

Cardinality

Cardinality restricts the volume of referenceability for any given value. For example, for the targeted marketing system, we may expect to find between one and three addresses for a customer—no more and no less. Other relationships may be based on one-to-one, one-to-many (infinite), or zero-to-many. The zero-to-many is interesting because it allows for the entry of a product without a sale. There are reasonable conditions on the cardinality in this case, whereby these products would be "new" products—perhaps products with an entry date in the last 14 days only.

Subtype/Supertype

Subtype/supertype constructs may also be found in the model. For example, the target marketing system may represent a customer's marital status as married, divorced, widowed, or single. Different constructs may apply to each customer marital state, like former-spouse data is relevant for divorced persons or an employee may also be a customer. Since most

---

[2] This is prevalent in data warehousing data stores since database RI duplicates RI enforced via the ETL process, thus unnecessarily requiring additional hardware and processing time.

employees are not customers, we would not carry the customer fields for all employees, just for the few who are both.

Subtype/supertype bounds the states of a given business entity. The logical progression through the various states for a business entity (that is: prospect, customer, good customer, former customer) is another quality check.

Reasonable Domain

Reasonable domains for values are especially useful for analyzing numeric data, whose data types can allow an enormous range of values, only a subset of which are reasonable for the field. These include items like incomes >$2,000,000 or <0; and offers mailed >1,000,000 or <1.

Valid values for credit scores is another example. FICO range is 300 to 900 and values outside of this range would be consider unreasonable and quite possibly incorrect. That's why we want to flag them for investigation.

Multiple Meaning Columns

Data columns should not be used for multiple meanings. Data types constrain the values in a column—to a degree. Any mix of 0 to 20 characters can go into a character (20) data type column. However, if this is a Name field, there are some sequences that you do not expect to find, such as all numbers, which may indicate the field is occasionally being used for a separate meaning. The field is flagged as containing inappropriate data.

Formatting Errors

There are various formatting errors that can be found in the field. Typical formatting errors found in name columns include, for example:
- A space in front of a name
- Two spaces between first and last name and/or middle initial
- No period after middle initial
- Inconsistent use of middle initial (sometimes used, sometimes not)
- Use of ALL CAPS
- Use of "&" instead of "and" when indicating plurality
- Use of a slash (/) instead of a hyphen (-)

In environments where original data entry is free-form, unconstrained, and without the use of master data as a reference, many of the violations mentioned above will be found.

Optional Data

Another type of typical data quality error involves columns that should only contain data if certain data values (or null) are present elsewhere. For example, in the customer table where some customers are organizations and others are individuals, only organizations have SIC codes, organization size, and so on (unless the presence of that data actually represents data for the individual's organization).

Derived Data

Some systems derive data from data in other systems. For example, one system may contain discount amount, unit price, and the discount percentage—a simple division calculation. Checking the veracity of calculations done in other systems is a common quality check.

Complete Data

The existence of data consistently through all of its history, without gaps, indicates users are not left to wonder what happened during missing periods—another common quality check.

Incorrect Data

There can also be incorrect data—for example, the inconsistent use of initials and misspellings or inappropriate spellings (such as William McNight instead of William McKnight).

Data Codification

Finally, does the data conform to the expected set of "clean" values for the column? For example, in the gender column we expect to find M, F, U (unknown), or the like.

Data quality rule determination determines the rules that govern our data.

Data Profiling

Hopefully categorizing data quality like this takes a bit of a load off. You have a list of categories of violations come from to review in conjunction with the data steward(s) and, eventually, the data itself.

Once the rules are determined, it's time to check them against the data itself in a process known as Data Profiling. Rules are chosen based on the business impact of the violation. Judgment needs to be used in determining the rules that you will take action on. In Profiling, for example, you may learn that an important rule is not being violated, so you would not choose to take action on it. Depending on the depth of the data quality problem and considering agile principles (Chapter 16), actions, themselves, should be staggered into the environment.

To enforce the "new" business rules consistently across all the data will require a cleanup effort. This brings us to the starting gate for making physical changes to the data to improve enterprise data quality.

Existing structures and their data must be analyzed to fit into the environment after the modeling cures are applied. It is highly desirous that the data quality be consistent across all history and into the future. This means remedying historical data (defined as pre-cleansing modeling) to the go-forward standard. This also can mean a set of challenges.

If, for example, you want to constrain future data entry for last names to be at least 2 characters, but you have several that are only 1 character today, something must be done with that data to bring it to standard. If, for example, you wanted to constrain future birthdates to be less than the system date, but you have several that indicate a birth year of 2099, what are you going to do with that data?

When there are fields like name in a customer record that, if incomprehensible, would invalidate the rest of the record, you cannot just nullify the data. There is a level of poor quality data, such as name of "xxx" that leaves you with nowhere to go with it by itself. From here, you can:

1. Give up and delete the record
2. Salvage the rest of the record (if it's of high quality) by making the name something like "Unknown"[3]
3. Pass the entire record to a human, who can do research with the other fields to come up with the name

No one field's fate should necessarily be decided based solely on that field's value. The adjacent fields should be considered as well.

There are other fields that you would expend less energy on getting correct. One key overriding principle in data quality is that you will never get it 100% perfect. You must balance perfection against timelines, budget, and value of the improvement of the data. A field like *automobile make* may not only be only mildly interesting, it may also be impossible to ascertain should the value be "xxx." For those invalid fields, you would nullify them.

You will never get data quality 100% perfect

---

[3] While carrying the poor quality data in a separate column or table for reference

When developing the cleanup strategy, it is worth reiterating that the primary focus of the decisions in support of data quality should be the business interests. These are best represented directly by those in the business with daily, direct interaction with the data in question. This is a good quality for the data stewards to have.

Data profiling can be performed with software, but do not simply train the software on the data and say "have at it." Enter your rules. Find out which ones are being violated and to what degree. Data profiling can also be performed using SQL. GROUP BY statements can show the spread of data in any column.

For example, we may find that, despite desiring/anticipating birthdates between 1900 and 1999 in our B2C customer table, there are some birthdates of 1869, 1888, 2000, 2999, and 9999. If data entry is unconstrained, as it often is, you will have these situations. Another example for consumer data entered online is a larger than expected number of consumers in Alabama, because it's the first choice on the list.

There are possibly some typos in this list (1869, 1888) but there is also some weirdness (2999 and 9999), which possibly indicates some rushed or lazy input. There is also 2000 which possibly challenges our assumption that we don't have any customer that young. Maybe we do. Maybe we let one through. Maybe the rule should be changed. Or maybe it's a valid rule and we want to know about any time it's violated. Remember, we are profiling in order to put into place rules that will be run on a regular basis on the data. We could do individual investigation on each violation, but it's more important to "stop the bleeding" going forward.

Many times, data quality work covers up for shortcomings in the originating systems. As master data management and other systems take up more data origination processes within organizations, information with better quality will flow into the organization.

SOURCES OF POOR DATA QUALITY

The following are seven sources of data quality issues.

1. **Entry quality:** Did the information enter the system correctly at the origin?
2. **Process quality**: Proper checks and quality control at each touchpoint along the path can help ensure that problems are rooted out, but these checks are often absent in legacy processes.

3. **Identification quality:** Data quality processes can largely eliminate this problem by matching records, identifying duplicates, and placing a confidence score[4] on the similarity of records.
4. **Integration quality:** Is all the known information about an object integrated to the point of providing an accurate representation of the object?
5. **Usage quality:** Is the information used and interpreted correctly at the point of access?
6. **Aging quality:** Has enough time passed that the validity of the information can no longer be trusted?
7. **Organizational quality:** The biggest challenge to reconciliation is getting the various departments to agree that their A equals the other's B equals the other's C plus D.

Master Data Management as a System of Data Origination

A growing source of important information in our enterprises is found in master data management (MDM) systems, which will be discussed in Chapter 7. Organizations are increasingly turning to MDM systems to improve data origination processes by utilizing MDM's workflow, data quality, and business rule capabilities. MDM systems provide for the management of complex hierarchies within the data, providing access to those hierarchies at any point in historical time.

If used as the system of origination or data enrichment, MDM systems generate the single version of the truth for the data it masters before any other systems gain access to the data. Then, those environments have systems that are working with the corporately adjudicated master data with high data quality, as opposed to environments in which each system is responsible for its own data.

This architecture can have a dramatic effect on enterprise data quality. However, the MDM environment must be modeled well in order to achieve the benefits.

You could be moving all kinds of interesting data around the organization with MDM, but if it does not adhere to a high standard of quality, it can all be for naught. Actually, that would be an MDM implementation that would not be worth doing at all.

Of course, again, the best place to ensure data quality is at the original point of entry. Remediation efforts after that point are more costly and less effective. Many data entry systems, even MDM, allow for free-form data entry, which is a real inhibitor to system success. The modeling may be more important in a MDM system than in any other system in the enterprise.

---

[4] Column indicating a measure of confidence (1–100) in another column of data

CURES FOR POOR DATA QUALITY

It is much more costly to fix data quality errors in downstream systems than it is to fix them at the point of origin. Primarily, if data entry in operational systems can be constrained to enter valid sets of values, this is a great help.

For example, if a name is being entered, automatic fill-in is a handy data quality assist. If a product is being entered, it should be from an up-to-date drop-down list. If appropriate, new data being entered can be compared against previously entered similar (including phonetically similar) data, and the entry function can be verified with "are you sure" type prompts.

If 50% of the data being entered into a field is unusable, our transformation strategy has no hope of salvaging much use out of this field. This is often the case with call-center data entry, where agents are rewarded based on the volume of calls taken. When this is the case, it's easy to ignore certain fields on the screen and accept the default (or worse—enter what's convenient but incorrect).

Fixing early entry systems is not always possible since many organizations deal with complex, older technology operational systems that are not easily changed. Many of these systems were written without an understanding of data quality or to provide data quality based solely on the operational purpose of the systems. Changing them takes many months and may involve a major cross-functional effort. Downstream systems, such as data warehouses, benefit from quality improvement in systems that improve the quality at the point of origin.

Wherever the changes need to take place, there is a reasonable set of actions that can be performed on data to increase its quality:

- **Hold Out**: Record(s) that are brought into the environment from other environments are held out of the main data areas in cases of gross rule violation. They may be placed into "holding" tables for manual inspection and action. If adapting this approach, be sure procedural reviews are held quickly, because data is held out of the system until it is accounted for.
- **Report on It**: Data quality violation is reported on, but data is loaded and remains in the data store for the system. Typically the handling of these violations involves nothing more than a post-load report on just-loaded data that creates visibility into the situation. These reports are not useful unless they are reviewed from the appropriate systems and by business personnel.
- **Change Data**: Transform data to a value in a master set of "good" values (for example, Texus is changed to Texas) or otherwise apply rules to improve the data.

It is also quite possible that referential sets of data, not singular rows, are affected when other forms of data quality defects are detected, and the appropriate action should be taken on that data as well as the data directly affected by the quality defect. As with all data quality checks, the data just loaded is the only data that needs to be checked.

It used to be that operational systems were hands–off to any interests beyond support of quick data entry. Well-intended speedup measures like removing drop-down lists and referential integrity had the predictable knock-on effect of lowering overall data quality. When the organization's lifeblood was the speed of those transaction entries, that made sense. Now that information is the battleground, that strategy, in isolation, doesn't make sense. We must find ways to speed up transaction entry while providing data quality at the same time.

To those who are skittish about touching operational systems and performance, try harder. The ghost was given up far too easily in the past.

The major data modeling constructs relevant to data entry data quality, which tie back directly to the data quality defect categories are:

1. Uniqueness
2. Reasonable Domain
3. Referential Integrity
4. Completeness
5. Derived Data

Defaults and null constraints are usually more problematic to data quality when used than when not used because they allow for an abstract value (or null, which is no value) to be used in place of a customized, relevant value.

These major constructs relevant to data quality are enforced in the organization in its data models. Implemented data models are the most leverageable place in the entire architecture to enforce change. If you get the data model correct by following the above constructs, the data has a much higher chance of having quality. Get the data model wrong and you spawn innumerable downstream workarounds and organization gyrations that run cover for the model shortcomings.

Data Quality Scoring

Once the systems and the data quality rules are identified and the data is characterized, scoring the data quality needs to be performed. Scoring represents the state of the data quality for that rule. System scores are an aggregate of the rule scores for that system and the overall score is a prorated aggregation of the system scores.

Scoring is a relative measure of conformance to rules. For a given rule, it could be as simple as the percentage of opportunities for rule enforcement that are positively met. For example, if 94% of genders conform to the desired values, that score is 94%.

Since many of the results will (hopefully) be above 99%, to provide a higher level of granularity to the scoring, you may set a floor at 50 (or any number) and measure the adherence above that number. For example, using the gender example, the score is (94-50) / 50, or 88%, instead of 94%.

ACTION PLAN

- Survey and prioritize your company systems according to their use of and need for quality data
- Develop business data stewards—subject matter experts and extended information team members—for important subject areas
- Determine, with the data stewards, the rules the data should live up to
- Profile data against the rules
- Score the data in the system
- Measure impact of various levels of data quality improvement
- Improve data quality
- Review systems of data origination and consider master data management

CHAPTER FIVE

Columnar Databases

One twist on the DBMS that fits in the post-operational architecture is a columnar database. A columnar database is a relational DBMS, stores data in tables, and accepts SQL for interaction. There is, however, a twist to the story from there.

Columnar databases reduce the primary bottleneck in those analytic queries from Chapter 3: I/O. I/O is a bottleneck due to the inability of the pre-CPU layers of memory, L2 (especially) and L1 caches to throughput data rapidly. One of the primary reasons for this is that complete records are sent through the layers by row-based systems, which are designed to process rows instead of columns. The caches add a lot of processing value to the CPU operation by reducing the time to access data and removing this valuable component from processing would not be a desired goal of any system administrator. The time-consuming part of the operation is the reading of the data page in the first place. If you're interested in just one column, it would be great to be able to find a bunch of that column's values on the page, without having to skip over those other columns that aren't interesting.

While disk density has gone up significantly in the last 20 years or so, packing much more data down into smaller spaces, I/O is still limited by the physical head movement of the arm. Physics simply won't allow such a small component to move much faster without the arm flying right off its handle (which could ultimately be why solid state disk becomes the norm over time).

Other than the larger page sizes, our designs have not changed much over the years to accommodate this I/O-bound reality. We have tried to make the OLTP database more analytic with specialized indices, OLAP cubes, summary tables, and partitioning, but we would need hundreds of drives to keep 1 CPU truly busy in a robust, complex, utilized data warehouse environment. It's not feasible. Incidentally, because of this bottleneck, random I/O has sped up much more slowly over the years than sequential I/O, which doesn't require nearly as much head movement.

COLUMNAR OPERATION

iTunes Demonstrates how Columnar Databases Work

iTunes has taught us we can buy by the song and not necessarily the album. When I want just a few songs from an album, it's cheaper to purchase only those songs from iTunes that I want. This is analogous to the columnar database.

The major significant difference between columnar and row-based stores is that all the columns of a table are not stored successively in storage—in the data pages. This eliminates much of the metadata that is stored on a data page. See Figure 5.1. The columns are tied together as "rows" only in a catalog reference. This gives a much finer grain of control to the RDBMS data manager. The need for indexes is greatly minimized in column-based systems, to the point of not being offered in many.

Columnar databases know where all column values begin on the page with a single offset calculation from the beginning of the file. There is no value-level metadata. All column data stores keep the data in the same row order so that when the records are pieced together, the correct concatenation of columns is done to make up the row. This way "Santa" (from the first name column file) is matched with "Claus" (from the last name column) correctly—instead of matching Santa with Bunny, for example. Columnar databases match values to rows according to the position of the value (i.e., 3rd value in each column belongs to the 3rd row, etc.).

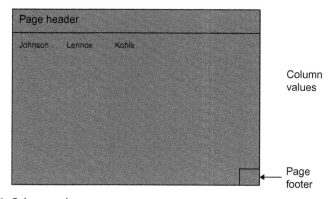

Figure 5.1 Columnar data page.

To optimize the I/O operation, it is essential to read as much as possible in each I/O. Many page sizes have been dramatically expanded in columnar systems from the typical 8 K/16 K/32 K/64 K you find in row-based relational systems.

●●●

Columnar databases not only provide higher amounts of data in I/Os but also higher amounts of "relevant" data in the I/Os primarily because they know all the data values must be processed that they read and the reads are less cluttered by page metadata for the DBMS' use.

An I/O in a columnar database will only retrieve one column—a column interesting to the particular query from either a selection or projection (WHERE clause) capacity. The projection function starts first and gathers a list of record numbers to be returned, which is used with the selection queries (if different from projection) to materialize the result set.

In row-based databases, complete file scans mean I/O of data that is nonessential to the query. This nonessential data could comprise a very large percentage of the I/O. Much more of the data in the I/O is essential to a columnar query. Columnar databases can therefore turn to full column scans much quicker than a row-based system would turn to a full table scan. Query time spent in the Optimizer is reduced as well, since this decision is not nearly as critical or fatal, if still less than ideal, to the overall query time.

COMPRESSION

The high likelihood of the same value being referenced successively on disk opens up a variety of unique possibilities for compression. Compression also greatly aids the I/O problem, effectively offering up more relevant information in each I/O. Below are some types of columnar compression. Please note not every columnar database will necessarily have every type of compression.

Dictionary Encoding

For fields above a certain number of bytes (and variable-length characters), a separate dictionary structure is used to store the actual values along with tokens. These fixed-byte tokens are used in place of the value in the data page and allow the data page to continue to operate without value-level

Dictionary:
A, United States of America, B, People's Republic of China, C, United Kingdom
Data Page:
A,B,C,B,A,C,C,B

Figure 5.2 Dictionary and data page snippet showing country column data on a data page.

metadata. The higher the repeat level of the values,[1] the more space will be saved.

For example, A = United States of America, B = People's Republic of China and C = United Kingdom, could be in the dictionary and when those are the column values, the A, B, and C are used in lieu of the actual values. See Figure 5.2. If there are 1,000,000 customers with only 50 possible values, the entire column could be stored with 4 megabytes (4 bytes per value). Some DBMS implement dictionaries at a "file" level—on a somewhat smaller basis than the entire table.

Trim Compression

Insignificant trailing leading zeroes and trailing insignificant spaces from character fields are compressed out, furthering the space savings.

Columnar Compression Versus Columnar Storage
Some of these compression techniques can be utilized by DBMSs that are not necessarily storing the data in columnar fashion. Except for run-length encoding, these techniques are concerned with the *values* and not necessarily the storage. Columnar stores are generally better at columnar compression and overall compression. Having the values physically together makes the compression easier to do.

Run-Length Encoding

When there are repeating values (e.g., many successive rows with the value of '12/25/13' in the date container), these are easily compressed in columnar

---

[1] Or, put another way, the lower the cardinality.

systems, which uses "run-length encoding" to simply indicate the range of rows for which the value applies. For example, run-length encoding indicating the value of '12/25/13' applies to rows 123 through 145.

'12/25/13' 123–145

Delta Compression

Fields in a tight range of values can also benefit from only storing the offset ("delta") from a set value. Some DBMSs calculate an average for a container and can store only the offsets from that value in place of the field. Whereas the value itself might be an integer, the offsets can be small integers, which doubles the space utilization. Compression methods like this lose their effectiveness when a variety of field types, such as those found in a typical row, need to be stored consecutively.

The compression methods are usually applied automatically (if desired) to each column, and can vary across all the columns of a table based on the characteristics of the data in the column. Multiple methods can be used with each column as well—for example, run-length encoding on dictionary tokens. The compounding effect of the compression in columnar databases is a tremendous improvement over the standard compression that would be available for a strict row-based DBMS. This is due to the vastly increased likelihood of similar values in columns as opposed to entire rows. In the near future, I expect that the customer will be able to utilize increased knowledge of compression techniques and have more capability to override the DBMS compression selections.

WORKLOADS

Now that you have seen the physical differences of columnar databases, it should be clear that the workloads that will find their best platform in columnar are queries that access less than all columns of the tables it touches. In this case, less is more. The smaller the percentage of the row's bytes needed, the better the performance difference with columnar.

It's optimal for queries that need a small percentage of the columns in the tables they are in, but suboptimal when you need most of the columns, due to the overhead in attaching all of the columns together to form the result sets.

DBMS Adding Columnar Capabilities

Some relational DBMSs have added columnar capabilities, changing the fundamental structure of having all of the columns of the table stored consecutively on disk for each record. The innovation adds columnar abilities to a table, effectively mixing row structures, column structures, and multi-column structures directly in the DBMS. In conjunction with the DBMS' partition elimination features, this creates a combination row and column elimination possibility.

It will be an option in your DBMS soon, if not now, to put any column into columnar storage (its own storage) or collect it into grouping of columns (multiple columns that share the same storage). It will be a key information management design principle to make these allocations wisely. Since the storage represents I/O, group columns where the workload will access those columns together most of the time.

Columnar databases allow you to implement a data model free of the tuning and massaging that must occur to designs in row-based databases, such as making the tables unnaturally small to simulate columnar efficiencies.

WORKLOAD EXAMPLES
Support for Managing the Customer

Identifying a customer across a company requires multiple multi-way joins across the large customer base.

To achieve the necessary company-wide customer profile, comprising activity across all products and channels, data is continually matched, reconciled, and summarized in an organization. Columnar databases are very useful in matching long records by just the keys, a process that happens repeatedly in the customer matching process.

Once a holistic customer profile is determined, many benefits accrue. Accurate and comprehensive customer profiling is essential. The characteristics of high-volume, wide-record data and distributed data sets and profiles that need matching, create the most compelling industry case for columnar deployment.

In addition, with profiling, churn can be much better managed. Once the value of a customer has been determined, the corresponding appropriate level of activity can be undertaken to prevent that customer from churn. Churn patterns can be learned from the data and potential churn can be anticipated and an intervention can be performed.

Cross-company Consolidation

Time to resolution is critical for these functions in a communications company. Anything that improves time to resolution of a query across silos must be considered. Considering that the queries look across all the systems with wide transaction records, the ADB is the matching, profiling, and analysis engine of a modern communications company that understands the importance of information.

Fraud Prevention

Companies need to reduce the latency between analysis and when an action is taken. However, nowhere is this need more critical than in the area of fraud.

Fraud analysis, under a rules engine or using pattern analysis, is looking at a few variables in a sea of data.

Naturally, there are fraudulent patterns of activity. These patterns are continually being learned and tuned "after the fact" and returned to the systems that analyze transactions. However, fraud is not a one-size-fits-all. Customer profiles must be considered in the process of taking remedial, counterbalancing actions. What is fraud for one customer is neither fraud nor unusual for another.

The scan-type queries that fraud engines, whether developed in-house or executed by a data mining tool, execute continuously are ideal for columnar databases due to their need to pull specific information out of a wide transaction record.

COLUMNAR CONCLUSIONS

A table scan of all columns will perform best in a row-based database. However, just because the row-based DBMS decided to do a table scan does not mean one is necessary in a columnar database. This is *hugely important* when assessing a columnar database. Some row-based DBMSs will decide to table scan at 15% selectivity.[2] In a columnar database, it would only access those vectors containing the interesting columns. Single column scans can therefore be much faster in columnar.

For small databases, the performance differences are muted.

A single record retrieval is better in row-orientation, especially when there are a high number of columns in the table. If the workload is mostly point queries of full records, you will be better off in row-based.

---

[2] If it's estimated that >15% of the row's bytes are needed.

The bottom line is column selectivity. Where it is high, those queries will perform better in columnar. This also means that longer rows (thereby creating a significant granularity to query selectivity) would lend themselves to columnar.

Columnar databases provide a range of benefits to an environment needing to expand the envelope to improve performance of the overall analytic workload. It is usually not difficult to find important workloads that are column selective, and that therefore would benefit tremendously from, a columnar orientation. Columnar database benefits are exacerbated with larger amounts of data, large scans, and I/O bound queries. In providing the performance benefits, they also have unique abilities to compress their data.

 ACTION PLAN

- Investigate if your DBMS(s) have columnar capabilities.
- If there, group columns where the workload will access those columns together most of the time.
- Determine how much of each workload is column-selective, how column-selective they are, and the importance of those queries.
- Put column-selective, large (terabyte+) workloads on columnar databases or DBMSs with columnar capabilities.
- Keep an eye on the QR Code for this chapter. Initially, I will have it pointing to a comparison of three columnar approaches by vendors out there.

CHAPTER SIX

Data Warehouses and Appliances

● ● ● ───

Please note in this chapter, by necessity, I will break custom and name a few vendors. The variety of approaches for analytic databases demand some representative deployed examples to explain the concepts.

DATA WAREHOUSING

If your data warehouse is under-delivering to the enterprise or if somehow you have not deployed one, you have the opportunity to deploy or shore up this valuable company resource. As a matter of fact, of all the concepts in this book, the data warehouse would be the first entity to bring to standard. There are innumerable subtleties and varieties in architecture and methods. Many are appropriate in context of the situation and the requirements. I will certainly delve into my data warehouse architecture proclivities later in the chapter.

First, I want to explain that the data warehouse is an example of an analytic database. It is not meant to be operational in the sense of running the business. It is meant to deliver on the analytics discussed in Chapter 3 and reporting, whether straightforward in the sense of basic reports or deep and complex predictive analytics.

In this context, the data warehouse will be the generalized, multi-use, multi-source analytic database for which there may or may not be direct user access. This data warehouse distributes data to other analytic stores, frequently called data marts. The data warehouse of this book sits in the No-Reference architecture at the same level as many of the other analytic stores. It is possible for an enterprise to have multiple data warehouses by this definition.

You should primarily make sure the data warehouse is well suited as a cleansing,[1] distribution, and history management system. Beyond that, be prepared to supplement the data warehouse with other analytic stores best

───

[1] Per the standard from Chapter 4 on Data Quality.

designed for the intended use for the data. At the least in this, where possible, you want the smaller analytic stores to procure their data from the data warehouse, which is held to a data quality standard. Many times the non-data warehouse analytic stores will be larger than the data warehouse itself, will contain other data, and cannot be sourced from the data warehouse.

Companies have already begun to enter the "long tail" with the enterprise data warehouse. Its functions are becoming a steady but less interesting part of the information workload. While the data warehouse is still a dominant fixture, analytic workloads are finding their way to platforms in the marketplace more appropriate to the analytic workload.

When information needs were primarily reporting from operational data, the data warehouse was the center of the known information management universe by a long shot. While entertaining the notion that we were doing analytics in the data warehouse, competitive pressures have trained the spotlight on what true analytics are all about. Many warehouses have proven not to be up to the task.

And it's analytics, not reporting, that is forming the basis of competition today. Rearview-mirror reporting can support operational needs and pay for a data warehouse by virtue of being "essential" in running the applications that feed it. However, the large payback from information undoubtedly comes in the form of analytics.

Regarding the platform for the data warehouse, if the analytics do not weigh down a data warehouse housed on a non–analytic DBMS (not an appliance, not columnar, all HDD storage),[2] big data volumes will. As companies advance their capabilities to utilize every piece of information, they are striving to get all information under management.

●●●———————————————————————————————————————

One site's data warehouse is another site's data mart is another site's data warehouse appliance or analytic database. Get your terminology straight internally, but find a way to map to a consistent usage of the terms for maximum effectiveness.

———————————————————————————————————————

All these analytic stores need to go somewhere. They need a platform. This is the set of choices for that platform:

1. Hadoop – good for unstructured and semi-structured data per Chapter 11, a poor choice for a structured-data data warehouse

[2] This applies to implementations of DBMS that have these capabilities, but the capabilities are not enabled.

2. Data Warehouse Appliance – described in this chapter, tailor-made for the structured-data analytic store; can be the data warehouse platform for small-scale or mid-market warehouses; highly scalable
3. Data Appliance – described in this chapter; highly scalable; it wants your operational workload, too; can be the data warehouse platform for small-scale or mid-market warehouses
4. Specialized RDBMS – Some specialized RDBMSs are not sold as appliances, so I'm putting them in a separate category; good for the analytic workload; many of these are columnar, which is covered in Chapter 5

There is a platform that is "best" for any given analytic workload. While I'm at it, there is one vendor solution that is best as well. However, you can merge workloads, creating other workloads. So a workload is not a workload now really. The "not best" possibilities in a modern enterprise are very large for any defined workload. As one analytic leader told me last month, "There are a million ways that I can manage this data." That statement is not just hyperbole!

The goal is to get as close as possible to the best solution without losing too much value by delaying. "Analysis paralysis," as they say, is alive and well in enterprise architecture decisions! This book is meant to cut through the delays and get you into the right category as soon as possible. You can cut out many cycles with this information and set about making progress quickly. So how do we define that "best"/good/good enough architecture?

When making product decisions for an analytic environment, the database platform is of utmost importance. It should be chosen with care and with active discernment of the issues and marketing messages. The landscape for this selection has changed. It is now much more of a value-based proposition. The architectural offerings have moved beyond the traditional Massively Parallel (MPP) or Clustered Symmetric, which have been the standards for many years.

The platform decision could come about based on new initiatives. However, it is equally viable to reassess the platform when your current one is going to require major new investment or simply is not reaching the scale that you require. It is also prudent for every shop to periodically reevalute the marketplace to make sure that the current direction is the right one in light of the new possibilities. Now is a time when the possibilities, with data warehouse appliances, merit such a reevaluation.

You will create a culture around your selected platform. You will hire and train your team to support it. It will become the primary driver for hardware and other software selections. Your team will attend user group meetings and interact with others using the DBMS for similar purposes. You will hire consultancy on the DBMS and you will research how to most effectively exploit the technology. You will need vendor support and you will want the vendor to be adding relevant features and capabilities to the DBMS that are needed for data warehousing in the future.

- Scalable – The solution should be scalable in both performance capacity and incremental data volume growth. Make sure the proposed solution scales in a near-linear fashion and behaves consistently with growth in all of: database size, number of concurrent users, and complexity of queries. Understand additional hardware and software required for each of the incremental uses.

- Powerful – Designed for complex decision support activity in an advanced workload management environment. Check on the maturity of the optimizer for supporting every type of query with good performance and to determine the best execution plan based on changing data demographics. Check on conditional parallelism and what the causes are of variations in the parallelism deployed. Check on dynamic and controllable prioritization of resources for queries.

- Manageable – The solution should be manageable through minimal support tasks requiring DBA/System Administrator intervention. There should be no need for the proverbial army of DBAs to support an environment. It should provide a single point of control to simplify system administration. You should be able to create and implement new tables and indexes at will.

- Extensible – Provide flexible database design and system architecture that keeps pace with evolving business requirements and leverages existing investment in hardware and applications. What is required to add and delete columns? What is the impact of repartitioning tables?

- Interoperable – Integrated access to the web, internal networks, and corporate mainframes.

- Recoverable – In the event of component failure, the system must keep providing to the business. It also should allow the business to selectively recover the data to points in time – and provide an easy-to-use mechanism for doing this quickly.

- Affordable – The proposed solution (hardware, software, services) should provide a relatively low total cost of ownership (TCO) over a multi-year period.

- Flexible – Provides optimal performance across the full range of normalized, star, and hybrid data schemas with large numbers of tables. Look for proven ability to support multiple applications from different business units, leveraging data that is integrated across business functions and subject areas.
- Robust in Database Management Systems Features and Functions – DBA productivity tools, monitoring features, parallel utilities, robust query optimizer, locking schemes, security methodology, intra-query parallel implementation for all possible access paths, chargeback and accounting features, and remote maintenance capabilities.

And then there's price. For the cost of storing data (i.e, a certain number of terabytes)—which is a lousy way of analyzing a workload[3]—Hadoop is going to be the cheapest, followed by the data warehouse/data appliance or specialized RDBMS, followed by the relational database management system. Functionality follows price.

There are many pitfalls in making this determination, not the least of which is the tendency to "over-specifying" a platform to account for contingencies.[4] Many appliances sell in a stepwise manner such that you buy the "1 terabyte" or "10 terabyte," etc. model. Overspecing an appliance can quickly obviate its cost advantage over the RDBMS.

What are we procuring for?

I used to recommend the procurement of a system that will not have to be altered, in terms of hardware, for 3 years. The pace of change has increased and I now recommend procuring for a period of about 1 year. In other words, you should not have to add CPU, memory (RAM), disk, or network components for 1 year. This is a good balance point between going through the organizational trouble to procure and add components and keeping your powder dry for market change, advancement, and workload evolution. If your system is in the cloud, providing rapid elasticity, this concern is passed to the cloud provider, but you still need to be on top of this.

Since the price of these systems is highly subject to change, I will seek to share specific information on pricing in this chapter's QR Code.

---

[3] Cost per gigabyte per second is a better technical measure.
[4] I've had clients who have had 3 levels of management increase the spec "just in case"—a problem somewhat mitigated by cloud architectures.

Tips for Getting the Best Deal
- Care about what matters to your shop
- Do all evaluations onsite
- Use your data in the evaluations
- Competition is key, do not tell vendor they have been selected until after commercials are agreed
- Don't share weightings with vendor
- Maintenance runs approximately 20% and is negotiable
- Care about Lifetime Cost!
- Offer to be a public reference, it's a useful bargaining chip
- Long-term relationship is important
- Don't try to shaft the vendor, spread good karma
- Best time to negotiate (especially with a public company) is quarter- and year-end

Even if your store is in the "cloud," you MUST choose it wisely. Being "in the cloud" does not absolve you from data platform selection.

Data Warehouse Architecture

No matter where you put your data warehouse, your decision points have only begun if you say you are doing an "Inmon"[5] or "Kimball"[6] data warehouse.[7] As a matter of fact, this "decision" can be a bit of a red herring and can impede progress by giving a false illusion of having everything under control.

Here are some of the post-Inmon/Kimball decisions that must be made for a data warehouse:
- Build out scope
- Business involvement
- Definition of data marts – units of work or physical expansiveness of use with ETL tool in ETL
- Processes data access options and manner of selection – by use, by enterprise, by category

[5] Bill Inmon, the "father of the data warehouse" and a proponent of up-front planning.
[6] Ralph Kimball, author of "The Data Warehouse Toolkit," known for dimensional modeling and expanding the data warehouses incrementally.
[7] Most common vendor mistruth is a variant of "just throw all your data on our platform and everything will be fine."

- Data retention and archival definition of data marts – units of work or physical expansiveness of use of ETL tool in ETL processes
- Granularity of data capture integration strategy – virtual and physical metadata handling modeling technique(s) need, utility, and physical nature of data marts
- Operational reporting and monitoring
- Persistence, need, and physical nature of data staging
- Physical instantiation of operational data stores – single-source, multi-source
- Program development team engineering technology selection process – framework, best-of-breed
- Source work effort distribution – source team, data warehouse team, shared
- Use of operational data stores for source systems – selective, complete

---

●●●

The best approach is an enterprise architecture that includes a strong data warehouse built with an agile development methodology with some up-front work and use of standards, broadly defined enterprises and virtualization techniques used to unite multiple enterprises.

THE DATA WAREHOUSE APPLIANCE

The data warehouse appliance (DWA) is a preconfigured machine for an analytic workload. Despite the name "data warehouse" appliance, as mentioned before, the DWA makes good sense for a general purpose data warehouse when the Achilles heels of the DWA, discussed later, are acceptable.

Non-data warehouse analytic workloads, however, are usually totally appropriate for a data warehouse appliance, a data appliance, or a specialized analytic store.

The data warehouse machine preconfiguration concept is not new. Teradata, Britton Lee, and Sequent are late 1980s examples of this approach. Hardware and software vendors have commonly preconfigured hardware, OS, DBMS, and storage to alleviate those tedious commodity tasks (as well as the risk of not getting it right) from the client. Well-worn combinations such as those put forward for TPC benchmarks are available from either the hardware or software vendor (to "ready prompt") in most cases. However, some of the new aspects of the modern data warehouse appliance are the use of commodity components and open source DBMS (or, in vendor terms, DBMS alternatives) for a low total cost of ownership. These open source DBMSs provide a starting point for basic database functionality and the appliance vendors focus on data warehouse-related functionality enhancements.

The current parallel RDBMS developments had their origins in 1980s university research on data partitioning and join performance. Resultant data movement or duplication to bring together result sets can be problematic, especially when gigabytes of data need to be scanned.

Analytic platforms, including data warehouses, have gone through phases over the years, including Symmetric Multiprocessing, Clustering, and Massively Parallel Processing.

Symmetric Multiprocessing

One of the early forms of parallel processing was Symmetric Multiprocessing or SMP. The programming paradigm was the same as that for uniprocessors. However, multiple CPUs could share the load using one or more of the forms of parallelism. A Least Recently Used (LRU) cache, kept in each CPU, makes this option more viable. SMP tended to hit a saturation point around 32–64 CPUs, when the fixed bandwidth of the bus became a bottleneck.

Clustering

Clustering became a way to scale beyond the single node by using an interconnect to link several intact nodes with their own CPUs, bus, and RAM. The set of nodes is considered a "cluster." The disks could either be available to all nodes or dedicated to a node. These models are called "shared disk" and "shared nothing" respectively. This was great for fault tolerance and scalability, but eventually the interconnects, with their fixed bandwidth, became the bottleneck around 16–32 nodes.

Massively Parallel Processing

Massively Parallel Processing, MPP, is essentially a large cluster with more I/O bandwidth. There can be up to thousands of processors in MPP. The nodes are still either shared disk or shared nothing. The interconnect is usually in a "mesh" pattern, with nodes directly connected to many other nodes through the interconnect. The MPP interconnect is also faster than the Clustered SMP interconnect. Remote memory cache, called NUMA (non–uniform memory access), was a variant introduced to MPP. DBMSs quickly adopted their software for MPP, and while the interconnect bottleneck was eroding, MPP became a management challenge. And it is expensive.

We can see that each step was an evolutionary advancement on the previous step.

●●●──

A data warehouse appliance is a preconfigured hardware, operating system, DBMS, storage, and the proprietary software that makes them all work together.

──

It became apparent that a real analytic workload could go beyond MPP with a strong price-performance push. Thus the data warehouse appliance was born. I call it "MPP Plus" because each appliance is based on MPP, but adds to it in divergent ways. I'll now showcase 3 data warehouse appliances (actually 1 DWA and 2 families of DWAs) to demonstrate the "plus" in "MPP plus." These are only meant as examples of the divergence of approach in data warehouse appliances.

IBM Netezza Appliances

IBM's Netezza is a leading data warehouse appliance family. Their preconfigurations range from 1 TB to multi-petabytes of (compressed) data. Netezza's philosophy is that parallelism is a good thing and they take parallelism to a new level. They utilize an SMP node and up to thousands of single-CPU SPUs ("snippet processing units") configured in an MPP arrangement in the overall architecture, referred to as "AMPP" for asymmetric massively parallel processing. The SPUs are connected by a Gigabit Ethernet, which serves the function of the interconnect.

There are hundreds of SPUs in a rack. Each rack fully populated contains a few terabytes. The racks stand over 6' tall. The DBMS is a derivative of Postgres, the open source DBMS, but has been significantly altered to take advantage of the performance of the architecture.

What's inside are multi-way host CPUs and a Linux Operating System. These are commodity class components and this is where the cost savings to a customer come from. Cost savings can also come from the lowered staff requirements for the DBA/System Administration roles. The use of commodity components is one important introduction from Netezza.

The architecture is a shared nothing, but there is a major twist. The I/O module is placed adjacent to the CPU. The disk is directly attached to the SPU processing module. More importantly, logic is added to the CPU with a Field Programmable Gate Array (FPGA) that performs record selection and projection, processes usually reserved for relatively much later in a query cycle for other systems. The FPGA and CPU are physically connected to the disk drive. This is the real key to Netezza query performance success—filtering at the disk level. This logic, combined with the physical proximity, creates an environment that will move data the least distance to satisfy a query. The SMP host will perform final aggregation and any merge sort required.

Enough logic is currently in the FPGA to make a real difference in the performance of most queries. However, there is still upside with Netezza as more functionality can be added over time to the FPGA.

All tables are striped across all SPUs and no indexes are necessary. Indexes are one of the traditional options that are not provided with Netezza. All queries are highly parallel table scans. Netezza will clearly optimize the larger scans more. Netezza does provide use of highly automated "zone map" and materialized view functionality for fast processing of short and/or tactical queries.

Teradata Data Warehouse Appliances

Teradata has taken its database management system and rolled it into a family of data warehouse appliances.

Teradata appliances utilize the Teradata DBMS. Throughout Teradata's existence, their solutions have been at the forefront of innovation in managing the tradeoffs in designing systems for data loading, querying, and other maximizing.

One of the keys is that all database functions in Teradata (table scan, index scan, joins, sorts, insert, delete, update, load, and all utilities) are done in parallel all of the time. All units of parallelism participate in each database action. There is no conditional parallelism within Teradata.

Also of special note is the table scan. One of Teradata's main features is a technique called synchronous scan, which allows scan requests to "piggy back" onto scans already in process. Maximum concurrency is achieved through maximum leverage of every scan. Teradata keeps a detailed enough profile of the data under management that scans efficiently scan only the limited storage where query results might be found.[8]

---

[8] "Teradata Intelligent Scanning."

The Teradata optimizer intelligently runs steps in a query in parallel wherever possible. For example, for a 3-table join requiring 3 table scans, Teradata starts all three scans in parallel. When scans of tables B and C finish, it will begin the join step as the scan for table A finishes.

Teradata systems do not share memory or disk across the nodes, the collections of CPU, the memory, or the bus. Sharing disk and/or memory creates overhead. Sharing nothing minimizes disk access bottlenecks.

The Teradata BYNET, the node-to-node interconnect, which scales linearly to over a thousand nodes, has fault-tolerant characteristics that were designed specifically for a parallel processing environment.

Continual feeding without table-level locks with Teradata utilities can be done with multiple feeders at any point in time. And again, the impact of the data load on the resources is customizable. The process ensures no input data is missed regardless of the allocation.

Teradata appliances use the same DBMS as Teradata's other DBMS.

The Teradata Data Warehouse Appliance

The Teradata Data Warehouse Appliance is the Teradata appliance family flagship product. With four MPP nodes per cabinet and scaling to many cabinets with over a dozen terabytes each, the Teradata Data Warehouse Appliance can manage up to hundreds of terabytes.

The Teradata Data Warehouse appliance can begin at 2 terabytes of fully redundant user data on 2 nodes and grow, node-by-node if necessary, up to dozens of nodes. The nodes can be provided with Capacity on Demand as well, which means the capacity can be configured into the system unlicensed until it is needed.

The Teradata Data Mart[9] Appliance

The Teradata Data Mart Appliance is a single node, single cabinet design with a total user data capacity of single-digit terabytes. It is a more limited capacity equivalent of the Teradata Data Warehouse Appliance, limited to that single node. So, likewise, it is suitable for the workload characteristics of an analytic that will not exceed this limit.

It should be noted that a single node environment comes with the potential for downtime in the unlikely event that the node fails—there is no other node to cover for the failure.

---

[9]Data "Mart" (vs. Warehouse) is a product label only and is meant to address scale of the project and not refer to the "polar opposite" of a Data Warehouse.

The Teradata Extreme Data Appliance

The Teradata Extreme Data Appliance is part of the Teradata appliance family. It outscales even the Teradata Active Enterprise Data Warehouse (Active EDW) machine, into the petabytes. A system of this size would have less concurrent access requirements due to the access being spread out across the large data. The Teradata Extreme Data Appliance is designed with this reality in mind.

It is designed for high-volume data capture such as that found in clickstream capture, call detail records, high-end POS, scientific analysis, sensor data, and any other specialist system useful when the performance of straightforward, nonconcurrent analytical queries is the overriding selection factor. It also will serve as a surrogate for near-line archival strategies that move interesting data to slow retrieval systems. The Extreme Data Appliance will keep this data online.

ParAccel Analytic Database

As a final example of how vendors are delivering data warehouse appliances, here is a little information about the ParAccel Analytic Platform from Actian Corporation.

ParAccel has elements of many of the above platform categories in one platform.

ParAccel is a columnar database (discussed in Chapter 5.) Being columnar with extensive compression, which packs the data down on disk, strongly minimizes the I/O bottleneck found in many of the contenders for the analytic workload.

ParAccel architecture is shared-nothing massively-parallel, the scalable architecture for the vast majority of the world's largest databases.

Another aspect of ParAccel is that ParAccel allows for full SQL. It also allows for third-party library functions and user defined functions. Together, these abilities allow a ParAccel user to do their analytics "in database," utilizing and growing the leverageable power of the database engine and keeping the analysis close to the data. These functions include Monte Carlo, Univariate, Regression (multiple), Time Series, and many more. It is most of the functionality of dedicated data mining software.

Perhaps the feature that makes it work best for analytics is its unique accommodation of Hadoop. Without the need to replicate Hadoop's enormous data, ParAccel treats Hadoop's data like its own. With a special connector, ParAccel is able to see and utilize Hadoop data directly. The queries it executes in Hadoop utilize fully parallelized MapReduce. This supports the information architecture, suggested below, of utilizing Hadoop for big data, ParAccel for analytics, and the data warehouse for operational support. It leverages Hadoop fully without performance overhead.

Connectors to Teradata and ODBC also make it possible to see and utilize other data interesting to where the analytics will be performed.

ParAccel offers "parallel pipelining" which fully utilizes the spool space without pausing when a step in the processing is complete. ParAccel is compiled architecture on scale-out commodity hardware. With in-memory and cloud options, a growing blue-chip customer base, and most importantly, a rich feature base for analytics and integration with Hadoop, ParAccel is built to contend for the analytic workload.

Achilles Heels of the Data Warehouse Appliance

The discussion of data warehouse appliances would not be fully wrapped up without noting some common Achilles heels. I want to be sure you understand them. I have said the (non-appliance) RDBMS is generally the most expensive form of storage. It requires more manpower than the appliance and is slower. I've said the appliance is "MPP Plus" and the installation is easier.

Data warehouse appliances' Achilles heels include:
* Concurrency issues
* Not designed to play the role of a feeding system to downstream stores
* Restrictions in upgrading; need to upgrade stepwise
* Lack of openness of the platform[10]
* Lack of redeployability of the platform to broad types of workloads
* False confidence in "throwing data at the platform" working out well

These are not uniformly true for all appliances, of course. However, these are very important to understand, not only in potentially eliminating them as the data warehouse platform, but also in making sure the "mart" workload is not encroaching on these limitations.

DATA APPLIANCES AND THE USE OF MEMORY

Finally, there is an even newer class of appliances, which don't conform well to a single label. I'll call them Data Appliances since they are intended to support operational as well as analytical workloads, unlike the

---

[10] I didn't want to say "proprietary" but many will for this Achilles heel; "commodity components" aside, some configurations make third-party support more difficult.

ill-named Data Warehouse Appliance. These Data Appliances are relational database machines that run databases. The Oracle Exadata Machine[11] and SAP HANA are the most prominent examples and are likely to be centerpiece examples of this approach to data management for decades to come.

While they both approach the challenge of data storage from a non-HDD perspective, they do it differently. HAHA is an all in-memory appliance (disk used for failover) whereas Exadata runs the Oracle DBMS on an intelligently combined SSD and in-memory platform with high amounts of SSD cache.

Innovation has occurred in multiple areas such as:

- Hardware innovations such as multi-core processors that truly maximize the value of hardware
- Faster analytics—faster access to complex calculations that can be utilized in support of immediate and appropriate business action
- The price of memory has precipitously dropped

The result of the innovation is the ability to use "more of" something that we have used for quite some time, but only for a very small slice of data—memory.

In-memory capabilities will be the corporate standard for the near future, especially for traditional databases, where disk I/O is the bottleneck. In-memory based systems do not have disk I/O. Access to databases in main memory is up to 10,000 times faster than access from storage drives. Near-future blade servers will have up to 500 gigabytes of RAM. Already systems are being sold with up to 50 terabytes of main memory. Compression techniques can make this effectively 10x − 20x that size.

As with columnar capabilities, I also expect in-memory to be a much more prominent storage alternative in all major DBMSs. DBMS will offer HDD, SSD, and in-memory.

SAP BusinessObjects introduced in-memory databases in 2006 and is the first major vendor to deliver in-memory technology for BI applications. There are currently many database systems that primarily rely on main memory for computer data storage and few who would claim to be absent any in-memory capabilities and with a roadmap with near-term strong in-memory capabilities.

While you should never use a data warehouse appliance for an operational workload, a data appliance will be much more readily adopted for an operational environment than an analytic store. From an analytic

---

[11] Occasionally, Oracle will reject the appliance label for Exadata, saying it is an "engineered system."

store perspective, the data appliance may be a "piggyback" decision in the enterprise and useful when workloads are when real-time, delay-free access to data can be utilized and delays will have measurable negative impact on the business. Keep an eye on the QR Code for updates on In-Memory systems.

ACTION PLAN

1. Sketch your current post-operational environment, showing how the data warehouse is juxtaposed with data warehouse appliances, relational marts, Hadoop, and column databases
2. Analyze where the data warehouse, if it's on a traditional relational DBMS, has workloads that are not performing as well as needed; consider moving them off to a data warehouse appliance
3. Consider if a data warehouse appliance is appropriate for housing the data warehouse
4. Make sure the data warehouse is, at the very least, cleansing and distributing data and storing history
5. Is a data appliance on the horizon for handling a lot of enterprise storage needs and could that include the analytic workload?
6. Put those workloads where real-time, delay-free access to data can be utilized and delays will have measurable negative impact on the business in systems with a large component of in-memory storage

CHAPTER SEVEN

Master Data Management: One Chapter Here, but Ramifications Everywhere

The No-Reference architecture touted in this book needs to find common ways to address commonalities across the enterprise. We can talk about technical tools like data integration and data virtualization and the softer factors of environment support like data governance, but there is also the data itself. This is where Master Data Management (MDM) plays a role.

I will argue that MDM is much more important than it has been given credit for. The more heterogenous the environment becomes—and it should become pretty heterogenous—the more important threading common data elements throughout the environment becomes. Ten, twenty, or fifty versions of customer data, for example, are counterproductive. Actually, there needs to be a way that any set of data that is interesting to multiple applications can be shared.

Master Data Management is an essential discipline for getting a single, consistent view of an enterprise's core business entities—customers, products, suppliers, employees, and others. MDM solutions enable enterprise-wide master data synchronization.

●●●
___

Every application needs master data. The question is how well—for both the application and the enterprise—the application will get its master data. It's HOW, not IF.
___

Some subject areas require input from across the enterprise. MDM, in a process known as governance (not to be confused with enterprise data governance) also facilitates the origination of master data. Business approval, business process change, and capture of master data at optimal, early points in the data life cycle are essential to achieving true enterprise master data.

A form of master data management is to master it in the data warehouse. However, as information becomes your corporate asset and you wish to control and utilize it as much as possible, this form of master data management is seldom sufficient. Likewise, the enterprise resource planning (ERP) promise of everything in one system leads companies to think master data could be managed there. However, ERP manages just the master data it needs to function and lacks governance and strong real-time enterprise distribution capabilities. I've yet to meet the ERP project concerned with the enterprise as opposed to its own functions. True MDM takes an enterprise orientation.

MDM JUSTIFICATION

The most straightforward way to think about the economic payback of master data management is "build once, use often." Master data must be built for each new system. Systems routinely have up to 50% effort and budget directed toward collecting master data. When master data is built in a scalable, sharable manner, such as within a master data management approach, this will streamline project development time, reducing the time it takes to get new systems up and running. Reducing scope also reduces project risk.

However, having multiple systems working from the same master data is where the ultimate benefit comes from. This is far greater than the total cost of ownership (TCO) "build once" approach, but more difficult to measure. There are efficiencies that come about from elimination of the contention and correlation of numerous "versions of the truth." One former pre-MDM client used to spend 80% of their campaign development time poring through competing product lists to determine which one was the true list for the set of products to be promoted. This left little time for the value-added creativity of the campaign. It also elongated development cycles to the point at which time-to-market opportunities would routinely be missed. Clearing up a problem like this is measurable.

I have been speaking of MDM as a support function. That is, MDM is in support of other projects such as campaign management. However, MDM may actually be a prime enabler for many projects such as those centered on customer or product analytics. There is high value to having customer lifetime value calculated. It improves campaigns and customer management Also, there may not truly be a complete set of master data anywhere in the enterprise today—only bits and pieces here and there. MDM may be the mechanism for most effectively introducing master data into the environment, as well as leveraging it into many systems.

You may have a more nuanced situation, but justification will often have to tie back to one of these total cost of ownership or return on investment approaches. MDM actually addresses such a wide range of information and cultural issues that seldom are two business cases alike.

I have done business cases focused on the TCO aspects of MDM that will span several projects, on generating customer hierarchies so that customer organizations are understood for risk aversion, on cleaning up customer lists for marketing purposes, and on generating customer analytics for more effective marketing, among others.

A SUBJECT-AREA CULTURE

Master data management programs focus on the high-quality shared data that the organization needs in numerous systems. This data is grouped into subject areas and consequently the MDM culture is a subject-area culture.

●●●

Master Data will ultimately comprise a small percentage, perhaps 5% of the volume of all organizational data. It's quality data, not quantity data.

Customer and product are two popular subject areas for the MDM treatment. However, depending on your organization, customer and product may be too large to comprise a single subject area and both, and others, may need to be divided further into smaller, more manageable, subject areas. If you cannot master the subject area in 6 months or you cannot locate a single organization responsible for the data stewardship of the subject area, then you should break the subject area into multiple subject areas. For example, I have divided customer into domestic/international, into gold/silver/regular, and by product line.

In the early days of master data management software, customer and product spawned their own software categories and, consequently, there are quite a few constructs in master data management specific to these subject areas. You need to decide if you want to invest time in reengineering your business to the predefined constructs of the subject area intellectual property or if you want MDM to be a palette upon which you can model *your business* bottom-up.

Other common subject areas that are mastered with master data management are parts, vendors, suppliers, partners, policies, stores/locations, and sales hierarchy. In reality, the list is unbounded and you should let your business needs guide your program's definition of subject areas and rollout schedule. I'm continually amazed at what constitutes subject areas for MDM. Once you get started with MDM, as long as it is leverageable, you can repeat MDM across many (dozens) of enterprise subject areas over time.

MDM is an iterative program, rolled out across the organization over time. I recommend mastering by subject area, although it is also effective to master by complete systems, taking from them what they publish and providing to them what is available and interesting as a subscriber. Often, a combination is best. Regardless of the rollout strategy, you will want to choose subject areas for MDM that have the following characteristics:

1. High interest to the enterprise
2. High reuse potential across many systems
3. High difficulty assigning ownership—either no one wants it or too many want it
4. Diverse input to its build
5. Scattered pieces of data throughout the enterprise

These may sound like complicating factors, but without these kinds of data problems, MDM would not be needed. However, it is usually not hard to determine numerous subject areas which can benefit from the MDM value proposition. That's the easy part. The harder part is actually mastering them!

MASTERING DATA

Master data management is about "build once, use often." It is about providing the same corporately adjudicated, useful data to applications across the enterprise. I've emphasized the data sharing aspect of MDM and even the data origination aspects. However, not to be overlooked is the fact that the high leverage you get with MDM means a little investment goes a long way. That investment may include more complicated attributes than simple, core attributes that are one-to-one with the subject—like a customer's address. It may get into more complex analytical data like customer lifetime value. Such attributes can be calculated and continually maintained in the master data management hub. Such attributes can utilize whatever data is sent to the hub in the calculations. Data may be sent that is not even stored and made available otherwise. Transaction data, for example, is not master data in the sense of being data that MDM hubs can handle volume-wise for sharing to the enterprise. However, transaction data is key to many analytics. Advanced uses of MDM include transaction data in this way.

Regardless of what you are sharing via MDM, the whole idea is not without its challenges and obstacles. Cultures that are decentralized, and that further lack documentation, cross-departmental working relationships, metadata, and a consistent lexicon have challenges. These are not factors that should keep you from doing MDM. They do, however, dictate about half of the cost and length of projects.

The benefits of master data management are pronounced and evident and well worth pursuing for organizations pursuing the No-Reference, heterogenous architecture. Information is being recognized as a corporate asset and there is the need to have that data managed operationally, not just in post-operational data warehouses and the like.

Tangible technical benefits of MDM include (for each subject area):

1. A multi-application data model, scalable to the enterprise
2. Master data publish and subscribe (sources and targets) ability
3. As appropriate, workflow processes that support the origination, verification, matching, etc. of data (automated and with human intervention)
4. Improved data quality (see Chapter 4)

As I've said, it's not IF, it's HOW each application, and consequently the enterprise, will manage master data. A tool is not necessary, but the approach outlined here is. All the disciplines of data modeling, data integration, data quality, and workflow management are necessary in managing enterprise master data management. All are available with a robust MDM tool.

Keep in mind, however, that it's actually the intangible by-products of these deliverables that may be more impressive. These include the fact that many knowledge workers and their applications will be working from the same set of data. They will not have to "roll their own" haphazardly and with only local control and interest. As with most of the advice in this book, I don't believe it costs more to do it the "right" way. It does takes knowledge and effort directed in a specific fashion.

THE ARCHITECTURE OF MDM

MDM data is the organization's crown jewels. It can be housed in different structures mentioned elsewhere in this book, but one of the most prominent ones is the data warehouse. Often this is inadvertent. Many organizations are pulling together their master data in a data warehouse (perhaps without referencing it as "master data"), which, you will recall from Chapter 6 is batch-loaded and downstream from operations.[1] This approach will mostly be inadequate in the No-Reference architecture.

---

[1] There are some data warehouses out there with selective real-time data, which is great and may alleviate some need for a separate MDM hub, but realistically pursuing real-time data warehousing is less worth it than pursuing operational business intelligence, of which MDM is a part.

I support the data warehouse as a key component of the architecture, but it bears repeating here that the data warehouse remains important even though it may not be storing master data. The data warehouse still provides a remedy to the inability to access data in operational environments. It still provides integrated, historical, and high-quality data. With MDM in the mix, the data warehouse will actually *receive* the master data from MDM.

In regards to the earlier comment about transaction data, it could be the data warehouse where the detailed transactions are accessible. Analytics can be generated from these transactions and fed back into MDM, augmenting the base of data that is there.

A second strategy for MDM data involves simply identifying where it exists today in the operational environment and creating pointers to those systems collected in an MDM "hub," then leveraging the hub when master data is needed. For example, the system of record for the base product data may be the Product system. The product analytics system of record could be the Sales system, and the financials related to the product could be kept in Lawson. These 3 systems would be joined when a full and complete customer master record is needed. Each subject area would have its own strategy similar to this.

This "virtual" or "registry" MDM strategy is quickest to deploy because it involves no systemic data movement. This strategy, cannot have workflow components added to it to enrich the data because there is not a separate place to store enriched data. The presumption is that the operational systems

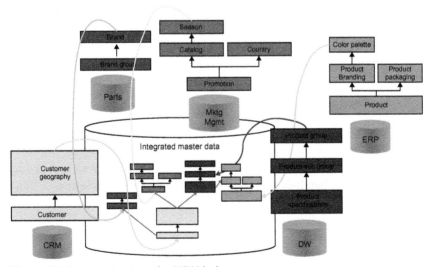

Figure 7.1 Getting data into the MDM hub.

are, in the aggregate, generating master data for the enterprise. Data quality is reduced to whatever occurs in the origination systems.

The bigger challenge with this approach is performance. To do cross-system joins on the fly for the customer, in the example, can be quite costly. Ultimately, it is most effective when limited sets of customer data are needed in the enterprise and data does not need to be moved systemically.

A better architectural approach for MDM, one that can support the No-Reference architecture, is to physically replicate the master data into a central hub and disperse it from there to other systems that need it. This separate physical hub exists in the architecture as a relational database, usually isolated, and maintained real-time for receiving published data and sending data that is subscribed to. This approach minimizes network traffic and system complexity. When master data is needed, it will be gathered from the MDM hub. Subscribers do not have to know where the data originated, although it may be communicated in the metadata for those who care.

Other value-added activity occurring at the MDM hub includes data cleansing, intake of syndicated data, and workflow execution for data origination and changes.

Data quality rules, such as those described in Chapter 4, should be applied to improve the data. Third-party syndicated data could be appended to the data at the hub. Workflows could be used to secure business governance to improve the data. Workflows could even be used to completely generate the master data and take the place of the originating "system-of-record" for the data in the architecture. For many implementations, this workflow/governance is the *main* value proposition for MDM. I will say more about the workflows in the next section, where it is referred to by its more common name of governance.

Third-party Syndicated Data

Data has existed for purchase for a while, but the data has mostly been sourced into a very specific need, such as a marketing list for a promotion. As organizations make the move to the leverageable data store that is MDM, an investment in syndicated data can be leveraged throughout the enterprise. With MDM, organizations have a system in which their efforts in data quality, sourcing syndicated data, and organizing a superset of attributes about important subject areas can be leveraged across the organization.

One big use of the syndicated marketplace is to augment and validate customer data and create prospect lists. Through a process called a reverse append, a small number of fields can go to the vendor and a very large number—of varying quality—can be returned.

The need for syndicated data has started many MDM programs since MDM is a central point for the collection and dissemination of master data.

Master data use tends to be very focused on distribution. However, there is a minor function for MDM data that, in certain shops, can become major. That function is the query of the data.

Master Data Query is also a function provided by MDM. MDM tools provide query "portals" to their databases. For some business functions, all that is needed is query access to the data. Implementations that focus on enriching raw data and turning it into analytics (see Chapter 3) for distribution can be referred to as Analytic MDM. Analytic MDM systems tend to have a higher interest in Master Data Query.

Most MDM is referred to as Operational MDM due to the focus on sharing consistent, clean information in real-time across the enterprise. Back to the notion that the value proposition for MDM is multifaceted, shops should drop this Analytical vs. Operational labeling and think about doing *both*. Analytic data is readily shared in mature MDM systems.

MDM GOVERNANCE

There are frequently manual aspects to the development of master data. We call these elements governance.[2,3] Each subject area has different requirements for MDM Governance. Some will need it for the complete build of the record from the very start through to completion. The screens used for the entry often resemble interactive dashboards or portals. Other subject areas will pick up incomplete records from systems and complete the record with governance. Others still will only use governance for a manual verification of the record.

The manual efforts are formed from workflow capabilities in MDM tools. For example, in order for a new product to be accepted into a retail operation, the Purchasing Manager needs cost, the Marketing Manager needs pictures, the Service Manager needs repair and warranty information, and the Training Manager needs features and benefits. Figure 1 is an example of a basic workflow.

[2]Note this is different from "data governance."
[3]Arguably, all MDM records could be considered "governed" since even those without MDM Governance form from confirmed sources.

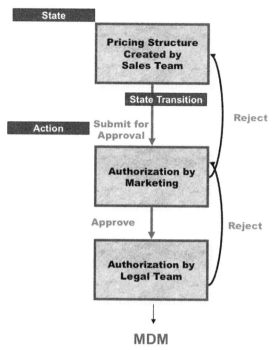

Figure 7.2 Master data management workflow.

Workflow is used to enrich the record, then "pass" the record from one person, department, or other collection of people as a group, to the next, perhaps going back and forth several times until the record is complete. The idea behind using a group is to have escalation and coverage and not have a dependency on a single person.

The flow can have all manner of forked paths, including parallel operations. The building blocks of the workflow are events, states, transitions, and users. The resultant actions from workflow events could be record manipulation or an email or a trigger event for organizational tasks in other systems. In the event of an unwanted delay, MDM workflow can re-prompt for action and even reassign tasks that are not getting executed. Within MDM, you define the escalation path and the time allotted at each person, ensuring (for example) new products continue to be introduced.

This process for getting to good records with governance is considered by many to be MDM's main value proposition. It is also frequently MDM's biggest challenge. It is for this reason, and others, that Organizational Change Management (see Chapter 17) is essential for MDM projects. Organizational Change Management's biggest value proposition to the No-Reference architecture is frequently in the area of MDM.

DATA QUALITY AND MDM

You could be moving all kinds of interesting data around the organization with MDM, but if it does not adhere to a high standard of quality, it can all be for naught. Actually, that would be an MDM implementation that would not be worth doing at all. Data quality is the absence of intolerable defects. Those defects are defined by the business and implemented with governance as well as data quality rules. Governance enriches data along the workflow. Data quality rules are applied in the hub to data as it enters and all the data disseminated has data quality.

MDM ROLES AND RESPONSIBILITIES

The business has major roles and responsibilities in MDM. The aforementioned governance process is one major example of this—both in the formation of the workflow, as well as being on the spokes of the workflow during its execution. We call both types of participants Data Stewards, as well as those contributing to the data modeling and data quality rules from the business side.

These senior business analysts in the subject areas being built into MDM should actually be considered part of the extended development team for the subject area they are the expert in.

There is also a Project Sponsor. This sponsor is ideally a business executive who understands the importance of information to the business and the importance of MDM to those objectives. The sponsor understands the short- and long-term capabilities of MDM in the organization and actively contributes to shaping them in the form of the iteration plan.

The sponsor will keep MDM out of internal cross-fire and chair recurring executive briefings on the project. They will chair the aforementioned data governance group and be the executive voice of requirements to vendors in the tool selection process.

MDM TECHNOLOGY

While MDM does not necessarily need a vendor-purchased tool, practically speaking it is difficult to pull off MDM without one. MDM tools coordinate all of the aforementioned functions without the need for disparate, discrete tools for each function.

Many vendors are claiming the MDM category and the large software companies have clearly positioned themselves in this space. You should base your shortlist on vendors who support the characteristics of your particular MDM need. Inevitably, given the breadth of MDM, every vendor will be providing many features that you would not consider important. Don't sell yourself short, though—those features may be prominent in your implementation someday.

Data quality tools may also be needed to address grievous data quality challenges above and beyond MDM data quality functions. Integration technologies such as an enterprise services bus, a data integration tool or some other manner of moving data will be necessary. Some MDM tools do not provide matching capabilities. Finally, syndicated data, naturally, is a separate purchase entirely.

ACTION ITEMS

- Divide your organization into its subject areas
- Prioritize the subject areas
- Determine the source(s) of record for each subject area for the new architecture
  - Determine which need governance, and to what degree
- Learn what is available in the syndicated data marketplace and develop a value proposition for syndicated data
- Assign value to the various components of MDM—data modeling, data integration, data governance, data quality

CHAPTER EIGHT

Data Stream Processing: When Storing the Data Happens Later

This is the real chapter on real-time access. It doesn't get much more real-time than sub-millisecond in-memory processing with Data Stream Processing. Data Stream Processing (DSP)[1] can hardly be considered a data store alongside the data warehouses, analytical appliances, columnar databases, big data stores, etc. described in this book since it doesn't actually store data. However, it is a data processing platform. Data is only stored in data stores for processing later anyway, so if we can process without the storage, we can skip the storage.

You will often hear DSP associated with data that is not stored. While it's not stored to facilitate the DSP, quite possibly we'll use DSP to process data because it's real-time and handles complex (multiple-stream) analysis and we'll still store it in a database for its other processing needs. Sometimes, however, the value of the data is primarily to serve DSP and, at hundreds of thousands of events per second, storing the data may not be needed.

The decision to process data with DSP and the decision to store the data in a database/file are separate decisions.

●●●

Data processed by DSP is increasingly best-fit in a Hadoop system given its high velocity and typically unstructured nature.

With permission, parts of this chapter have been pulled from "Stream Processing" by William McKnight, published on BeyeNETWORK.com. Read the full article at: http://www.b-eye-network.com/view/15968.

The information management paradigm of the past decade has been to capture data in databases to make it accessible to decision makers and knowledge workers. To reduce query loads and processing demands on operational systems, data from operational systems is typically transferred into databases where it becomes part of the information value chain.

[1] Also known as Event Stream Processing

In the value chain that leads from data availability to business results (data→information→knowledge→action→results), making data available to end users is just a part of the cycle. The real goal of information management is to achieve business results through data.

The information value chain is data→information→knowledge→action→results

One technology that has made that information more accessible, albeit in a different paradigm, is stream processing. With stream processing, and other forms of business intelligence known as operational business intelligence because it happens to data in operational systems, data is processed before it is stored (if it is ever stored), not after.

Data velocity can severely tax a store-then-process solution, thereby limiting the availability of that data for business intelligence and business results. Stream processing brings the processing into real-time and eliminates data load cycles (at least for that processing). It also eliminates the manual intervention that would be required if the data were just made available, but not processed.

Stream processing is often the only way to process high velocity and high volume data effectively.

Since all data can contribute to the information management value chain and speed is essential, many companies are turning to processing directly on the data stream with a process-first approach. It's more important to process data than store it; and with data stream processing, multiple streams can be analyzed at once. It has become very common to spread the operational workload around by processing different transactions of the same type in multiple systems. With stream processing, all of these streams can be processed at the same time. The added complexity of multiple streams is sometimes referred to as complex event processing (CEP),[2] which is a form of DSP.

Many organizations have redundant processing systems. Think of the systems financial services organizations have in place to process trades. Several trades executed by a customer could be processed on different

---

[2]Also known as Concurrent Stream Processing.

systems all over the world. Without CEP, it would be impossible to draw real-time inferences from these trades by the same customer.

CEP is looking across the streams for opportunities and threats.

USES OF DATA STREAM PROCESSING

Wash trades, which happens when an investor simultaneously sells and buys shares in order to artificially increase trading volume and thus the stock price, are illegal, as are many other simultaneous trades meant to overload a system and catch it unaware. It's not just good business practices and deterring fraud that are driving putting mechanisms in place to stop fraudulent trades. Regulations have also been created that impose this type of governance on financial services organizations.

According to the Wall Street Journal, "U.S. regulators are investigating whether high-frequency traders are routinely distorting stock and futures markets by illegally acting as buyer and seller in the same transactions, according to people familiar with the probes. Investigators also are looking at the two primary exchange operators that handle such trades, CME Group Inc., and IntercontinentalExchange Inc., the Atlanta company that in December agreed to purchase NYSE Euronext for $8.2 billion, the people said. Regulators are concerned the exchanges' systems aren't sophisticated enough to flag or stop wash trades, the people said" (Patterson et al., 2013).

CME Group, for example, famously has DSP technology: TIBCO Streambase (Schmerken, 2009). It will need to convince US regulators it is using it well to prevent wash trades.

●●●──

Financial services and capital markets companies are leading the charge into data stream processing, specifically complex event processing.

CEP allows a financial institution to look "across" all of its streams/ systems/trades simultaneously and look for patterns that can trigger an automated action. For example, it can look at a trader's complete set of trades for the last 5 minutes or for the last 30 trades, regardless of when they occurred. CEP can then look for the same security symbol in multiple trades or whatever indications in the transaction data should trigger action. Another common use is CEP looking at overall trader volume to determine if the trades should be allowed. Individuals can be grouped by association to determine fraud as well.

With customer profiling (see the chapter on Master Data Management), it can be determined what the normal behaviors of an individual and a peer group are. Hidden links between accounts and individuals can be discovered. For example, it may be determined that a broker may have multiple accounts in the names of several connected people.

This happens outside of DSP, but is used as supporting master data that triggers proper action within DSP.

Such actions resulting from DSP may include:

1. Cancelling the trade(s)—after all, it is not completely processed, yet
2. Postponing the trade(s) until a manual review is completed
3. Allowing the trade(s)

The primary actions you would seek from DSP (including CEP) are 1 and 2 above. If 100% of transactions fell to 3, this is not a good use of DSP. DSP is useful when immediate actions are necessary. When possible, you should allow the transactions to hit the database(s) from which they would be picked up—for example, by Master Data Management for distribution. It's more efficient.

The manual review will be used to determine intent and develop a case backed by data. The process needs to be executed quickly and efficiently.

A transaction contains various points of information that are interesting to feed to a Master Data Management hub (see Chapter 7). There is trade count, trade volume, updates to the trading profile, and an association between the trader and the securities. Once it gets in MDM, it is available for immediate distribution to the organization.

Every organization has data streams. It's data "in play" in the organization, having been entered into an input channel and in the process of moving to its next organizational landing spot, if any. Two fundamental approaches are taken with stream processing:

1. Gather the intelligence from the transaction
2. Use the transaction to trigger a business activity

Any data that needs to be acted on immediately should be considered for DSP. High-velocity actionable data is a good candidate for stream processing. Made possible by stream processing, the successful real-time intervention into any of these processes easily translates into savings of millions of dollars per year in large companies with high velocity/high volume transaction data.

Health-care companies can analyze procedures and symptoms and bring real-time useful feedback into the network immediately. For example, they can look for distribution of potentially incompatible drugs that are potentially being distributed in an emergency situation.

●●●
_____

The stream can often be visualized with the DSP tool.
_____

Retailers can make smart next-best offers to their customers based on what the shopper is currently (this moment) experiencing.

Manufacturers can detect anomalous activity on the production line such as changes in tempo, temperature changes, and inventory drawdown.

The U.S. Department of Homeland Security uses DSP to monitor and act on security threats by looking at patterns across multiple systems, including analyzing multiple streams of videos for suspicious simultaneous activity. DSP is also being used on the battlefield as well to spot impending danger based on the path of numerous objects.

Many types of organizations, including financial services organizations, can analyze streams from suppliers to immediately take up the best (least expensive) offers.

High volume trading can also use DSP to take advantage of opportune market conditions when every sub-millisecond counts.

Candidate workflows for data stream processing should be analyzed through the lens of the need for real-time processing. There are limitations as to what "other" data can be brought to bear on the transaction and used in the analysis. Integration cannot be physical. After all, these streams have high velocity, and real-time analysis has to be done on a continuous basis. As the worlds covered in this book (MDM, Hadoop, data virtualization, analytic databases, stream processing, etc.) collide, I expect that the MDM hub, containing highly summarized business subject-area information, will be the entity utilized with stream processing, possibly with data virtualization (Chapter 9).

Once you're incorporating other data in the analysis, from a risk perspective, organizations have more data to consider regarding whether a transaction should be or should not be allowed. While some transactions may appear to be risky, many others could appear to be suspicious only due to lack of an up-to-date customer profile, which increasingly will be in an MDM store. Regardless, the point is that it is very possible to combine stream processing with master data through data virtualization.

DATA STREAM PROCESSING BRINGS POWER

The business world is changing so fast. Those who can embrace the technological advances, regardless of company size, can certainly level the playing field. DSP brings this kind of power to all who embrace it.

For example, trading algorithms on Wall Street used to be developed over time and utilized for months or quarters. Today, traders need to be updating and applying change to their algorithms much more rapidly. Applying DSP can allow for these algorithms to be developed much more quickly and effectively. The key to algorithmic success is knowledge of DSP and the application of "data science," rather than being a Tier 1 bank. Also, similar to offer analysis, a trading firm can determine the best venue and method for executing their orders.

STREAM SQL EXTENSIONS

Stream processing accommodates an SQL-like programming interface that has extended SQL in the form of time series and pattern matching syntax that allows analysis to take place in "the last n minutes" or "the last n rows" of data. Processing a "moving window" of cross-system, low-latency, high-velocity data delivering microsecond insight is what stream processing is all about.

If you're used to SQL, you may be surprised at the conceptual similarities between a database and a stream from an SQL perspective. Essentially, the stream is treated as a table (referred to as a Stream Object) and the SQL extensions are extensions to basic SQL.

An important area of SQL extension is time series processing.

The high volume-trading customer's decision rule example could look like this:

WHEN ORCL price moves outside of its moving average by 4%
AND My portfolio moves up by 2%
AND IBM price moves up by 5% OR ORCL price moves down by 5%
ALL WITHIN any 3 minute interval
THEN buy 100 shares of ORCL and sell 100 shares of IBM

This example utilizes multiple streams (My Portfolio, ORCL share price, IBM share price). It includes the time series (within any 3-minute interval). The logic comprises events in multiple streams and the action to be done is automated: buy ORCL, sell IBM. Of course, this is pseudocode and DSP must actually send the buy and sell transactions to the trading system.

Imagine holding binoculars to watch the fish pass in several streams simultaneously. This represents the time orientation of DSP, since you can only see the last few seconds of activity in the lens.

A Fraud Detection System (FDS) could look like this:

IF the requested loan amount exceeds $100,000

AND a denied loan application exists for a similar name and address

ALL WITHIN any 2 hour interval

THEN display denial message on dashboard

In this case, you are using the time-series features of the StreamSQL extensions to advantage to encompass low-velocity data (loan applications) across a larger time period (2 hours). The only limitation on data within the analysis is the size of memory.

Smartphones currently pulse where you are every few seconds. If your company's app has location services turned on, you can use it to your advantage to monitor users' locations and cross-reference that to current promotions that may be of interest to the customer.

A Location Detection system might look like this:

IF I have an active promotion

AND we can detect customer location

AND customer is within 5 miles of a retail location

AND has purchased in the promotion's category in the last year

THEN send a text message with the promotion.

Tracking people is one thing—and a very profitable one at that. Tracking most everything else as well is referred to as the "internet of things." Based on its ability to look across streams and generate activity, DSP will play a huge role in this emerging movement.

IN CONCLUSION

Like columnar databases and data virtualization discussed in this book, DSP may or may not stand alone as a technology. Increasingly it is being embedded in other technologies and packaged applications—some described in this book and others in the category of Business Process Management (BPM). Regardless, DSP merits each shop, especially the information management architecture office, be well aware of the possibilities of DSP as a unique domain and put it to use when real-time and cross-stream processing matters and data storage may or may not matter.

ACTION PLAN

- Analyze workloads to determine which could provide more value if they were truly real-time
- Analyze the opportunities to look across streams of data to create immediate and automated actions
- Analyze the current toolset to determine what DSP capabilities you may already have

REFERENCES

Patterson, S., Strasburg, J., Trindle, J., 2013. Wash trades scrutinized. Wall St. J. March (17) <http://online.wsj.com/article/SB10001424127887323639604578366491497070204.html>.
Schmerken, I., 2009. CME group picks streambases CEP platform for options pricing. Wall St. Technol. June (23) <http://www.wallstreetandtech.com/electronic-trading/cme-group-picks-streambases-cep-platform/21810083>.

CHAPTER NINE

Data Virtualization: The Perpetual Short-Term Solution

One of the premises of this book is that information will, by necessity, be spread throughout the organization into heterogeneous data stores. While the allocation of data to a platform should be ideal for the *majority* of its usage, obviously the selection can never be perfect for *all* uses. Therein lies a dilemma. Physical comingling of data on a platform will always yield results with the highest performance.[1] The tradeoffs are the cost of redundant, disparate, and uncontrolled data. It's more than the cost of storage. People costs, error corrections, and faulty decision making because of disparate, errant data are far more costly.

One technology, or capability if you will, providing us the dilemma by providing query capabilities across platforms is data virtualization. Data virtualization is middleware that has less to do with the rendering of the result set and everything to do with the platforms in which the data resides—those platforms we are selecting from throughout this book. For these reasons, I discuss it in its own chapter and don't include it in the business intelligence chapter (Chapter 15).

With permission, parts of this chapter have been pulled from "Data Virtualization" by William McKnight, published on BeyeNETWORK. com. Read the full article at: http://www.b-eye-network.com/view/15868.

THE HISTORY OF DATA VIRTUALIZATION

Data virtualization is not new. It has been a capability out there for a long time. Historically, it has underperformed expectations and was used to circumvent moving data into the data warehouse that really should have been physically cohabiting with the other data warehouse data. The resulting cross-platform queries, built into the technical architecture, tended to be slow and bring dispute to the notion of a well-performing

---

[1] A consideration for cloud computing as well, covered in Chapter 13.

cross-platform query, which is needed much more today as organizations have a wider variety of heterogeneous platforms to choose from.

In the heyday of data warehouse building, data virtualization was pushed too hard and too fast and it got the proverbial black eye for trying to create the unworkable "virtual data warehouse." Difficult to consolidate, this style of warehouse left pieces around the organization and imagined a layer over all of them, stitching together result sets on the fly. In most cases, this was unworkable. The "hard part" of consolidation, ideally supported by governance, was required. It still is. You would not refrain from building a data warehouse and simply rely on data virtualization. For the reasons mentioned in Chapter 6, a data warehouse is still required. However, there are times today when data virtualization can be a short-term solution or a long-term solution.

Fortunately, the technology has caught up and deserves a second look. There are stand-alone data virtualization tools and some degree of data virtualization is built into many business intelligence tools and even platforms. Some of the latter tends to be more limited in focus on close technology partners to the technology.

Data Virtualization is an enabler of the No-Reference architecture.

CONTROLLING YOUR INFORMATION ASSET

Every organization should expect chaos over the next decade while working to get the important asset of information under control. Technical architecture will drag behind the delivery of information to users. Much of data delivery will be custom. Data virtualization will be useful in this custom, creative delivery scenario. It has the ability to provide a single view of data that is spread across the organization. This can simplify access, and the consumer won't have to know the architectural underpinnings. These are the short-term solution aspects to data virtualization.

How long is the short term? Term is a vague concept in this era of technological advancement, but nonetheless it is important to have time frames in mind for solutions in order to make wise investments. In the case of data virtualization, the short term is until the architecture supports a physical view through integration or until it becomes evident that data will remain consciously fragmented and data virtualization becomes the long-term solution.

The right architectural answer may be to not centralize everything, and the right business answer may be to not take the extended time to design and develop solutions in the three distinct technologies—business intelligence, data warehousing, and data integration—required for replicating the data.

Leveraging Data Virtualization

While many programs like the data warehouse, CRM, ERP, big data, and sales and service support systems will be obvious epicenters of company data, there is the inevitable cross-system query that must be done periodically or regularly. Many organizations start out by leveraging their data virtualization investment to rapidly produce operational and regulatory reports that require data from heterogeneous sources.

Further queries spawn from this beginning since data virtualization has the only bird's-eye view into the entire data ecosystem (structured/unstructured), seamless access to all of the data stores that have been identified to the virtualization tool, including NoSQL stores, cloud-managed stores, and a federated query engine.

As middleware, data virtualization utilizes two primary objects: views and data services. The virtualization platform consists of components that perform development, run-time, and management functions. The first component is the integrated development environment. The second is a server environment, and the third is the management environment. These combine to transform data into consistent forms for use.

Integrated Business Intelligence

Data virtualization is used primarily for providing integrated business intelligence, something formerly associated only with the data warehouse. Data virtualization provides a means to extend the data warehouse concept into data not immediately under the control of the physical data warehouse. Data warehouses in many organizations have reached their limits in terms of major known data additions to the platform. To provide the functionality the organization needs, virtualizing the rest of the data is necessary.

Pfizer and Data Virtualization

Pfizer had an "information sharing challenge" with applications that "don't talk to each other." They implemented data virtualization without sacrificing the architectural concepts of an information factory. Source data was left in place, yet all PharmSci data was "sourced" into a single reporting schema accessible by all front-end tools and users. The fact that data virtualization has the ability to cache data from a virtual view as a file or insert the data into a database table (via a trigger) adds significant value to the solution.

—Dr. Michael C. Linhares, Ph. D. and Research Fellow

The Pfizer head of the Business Information Systems team has a nice quote in the book "Data Virtualization" (Davis and Eve, 2011), which sums up much of data virtualization's benefits: "With data virtualization, we have the flexibility to decide which approach is optimal for us: to allow direct access to published views, ... to use caching, ... or to use stored procedures to write to a separate database to further improve performance or ensure around the clock availability of the data." Sounds like flexibility worth adding to any shop.

Data virtualization brings value to the seams of our enterprise—those gaps between the data warehouses, data marts, operational databases, master data hubs, big data hubs, and query tools. It is being delivered as a stand-alone tool as well as extensions to other technology platforms, like business intelligence tools, ETL tools, and enterprise service buses.

Data virtualization of the future will bring intelligent harmonization of data under a single vision. It's not quite there yet, but is doubtless the target of research and investment due to the escalating trends of competitive pressures, company ability, and system heterogeneity.

Using Data Virtualization

Data virtualization is a class of stand-alone tools as well as a significant capability added to many other tools, mostly database systems. It is important enough to understand discretely in order to get a full handle on information architecture. I will use "tools" generically to refer to a data virtualization tool or to the capability within a separate tool.

Something virtual does not normally physically exist, but based on the judgment of the tool and the capacity of its cache, the tool may actually physically create the desired structure. Regardless, at some point it has to "join" the data from the heterogeneous sources and make it available. Virtualization refers to querying data that is not guaranteed to reside in a single physical data store, but may as a result of caching. Check to see how intelligent the caching mechanisms of your chosen virtualization platform is. Some will rival the temperature sensitivity capabilities of a robust DBMS.

Checklist of Data Virtualization Tool Requirements

1. Data stores it can access
2. Intelligence in determining data for its cache
3. Optimizer's ability to manage the multiple optimizers of the data stores
4. User management
5. Security management
6. Load balancing
7. User interface

While some tools provide a user interface which is useful for those odd queries you may want to run, combining data virtualization with a business intelligence tool (or as part of a business intelligence tool) gets the virtualization capability into the tools that the users are used to for their single-system queries.

Use Cases for Data Virtualization

Given the heterogeneous information management architecture, the goal of eliminating unnecessary redundancy, and the capabilities of data virtualization, we land data in its best spot to succeed and go from there.

Data virtualization is not a materialized view, which is always a physical structure.

Data Virtualization Use Cases

Composite Software, a prominent data virtualization vendor and part of Cisco Systems, organizes the data virtualization use cases as follows:
- BI data federation
- Data warehouse extensions
- Enterprise data virtualization layer
- Big data integration
- Cloud data integration

There is some obvious overlap between these. For example, most data warehouses are built for business intelligence, so extending the warehouse virtually actually provides federation for BI. This form of virtualization is helpful in augmenting warehouse data with data that doesn't make it to the warehouse in the traditional sense, but nonetheless is made available as part of the warehouse platform. Big data integration refers to the integration of data in Hadoop, NoSQL systems, large data warehouses and data warehouse appliances. Finally, the cloud is presented as a large integration challenge that is met by data virtualization.

Master Data Management

Master Data Management (MDM), discussed in Chapter 7, is built for governing data and distributing that data. The distribution of MDM data has a significant architectural aspect to it. MDM data does not have to be physically distributed to a similar structure residing in the target system that wants the data. Depending on the frequency of access and the concurrency requirements on the MDM hub itself, MDM data can stay in the hub and be joined to data sets far and wide in the No-Reference Architecture. Ultimately, MDM will be the highest value usage for data virtualization.

When the structure you wish to join MDM (relational) data with is not relational, you may create a separate relational store for use with the nonrelational data (which would still necessitate data virtualization) or you can utilize the main MDM hub for data virtualization.

●●●

Data virtualization is not synchronization, which is keeping two separate data stores consistent in data content without much time delay.

MDM data can increase the value of Hadoop data immensely. Hadoop is going to have low granularity transaction-like data without information, other than perhaps a key, about company dimensions like customer. Those transactions can be analyzed "on the face" of the transaction, which has some value, but the value of bringing in information not found in the transaction—but relevant to it—is much more valuable.

If analyzing people's movements across the store based on sensor devices, while it's helpful to know a generic person's pattern, it is more helpful to know it is Mary Smith, who lives at 213 Main Street (an upper scale geo), has a lifetime value that puts her in the second decile, has two kids, and prefers Nike clothing. You can design the store layout based on the former, but you can make targeted offers, too, based on the latter.

A similar analogy applies to MDM and Data Stream Processing (Chapter 8), which has to do with real-time data analysis. Analyzing the stream (by human or machine) along with the dimensional view provided by MDM means you can customize the analysis to the customer, product characteristics, and location characteristics. While a $10,000 credit card charge may raise an alert for some, it is commonplace for others. Such limits and patterns can be crystalized in MDM for the customers and utilized in taking the next best action as a result of the transaction.

Data virtualization cannot provide transactional integrity across multiple systems, so data virtualization is not for *changing* data. It is for accessing data.

Because data streams are not relational, the MDM hub could be synchronized to a relational store dedicated to virtualization with the stream processing or the stream processing could utilize the MDM hub. The decision would be made based on volume of usage of the hub, physical proximity of the hub, and concurrency requirements to the hub.

Adding numerous synchronization requirements to the architecture by adding numerous hubs can add undue overhead to the environment. Fortunately, most MDM subscribers today are relational and have a place in the data store for the data to be synchronized to.

Mergers and Acquisitions

In the case of a merger or acquisition (M&A), immediately there are redundant systems that will take months to years to combine. Yet also immediately there are reporting requirements across the newly merged concept. Data virtualization can provide those reports across the new enterprise. If the respective data warehouses are at different levels of maturity, are on different database technologies or different clouds, or differ in terms of being relational or not, it does not matter. Obviously, these factors also make the time to combine the platforms longer, and possibly not even something that will be planned.

Data virtualization has the ability to perform transformation on its data, but—as with data integration—the more transformation, the less performance. With virtualization happening at the time of data access, such degregations are magnified. Approach data virtualization with heavy transformation and CPU-intensity with caution.

I am also using M&A as a proxy for combining various internal, non-M&A based fiefdoms of information management into a single report or query. While the act of an M&A may be an obvious use case, companies can require M&A-like cross-system reporting at any moment. This is especially relevant when little information management direction has been set in the organization and a chaotic information environment has evolved.

Temporary Permanent Solution

The need to deliver business intelligence per requirements may outweigh your ability to perform the ETL/data integration required to physically commingle all the data required for the BI. Any data integration requirements are usually the most work intensive aspect of any business intelligence requirement.

As you set up the information management organization for performing the two large categories of work required—development and support—you will need to consider where you draw the line. Development is usually subjected to much more rigorous justification material, rigorous prioritization, and project plans or agile set up. Support is commonly First In, First Out (FIFO), queue-based work that is of low scope (estimated to be less than 20 person-hours of effort).

Having run these organizations, I've become used to doing quick, and pretty valid, estimations of work effort. I know that when the work involves data integration, it likely exceeds my line between development and support, so I put that in the development category. Unfortunately, now that we can no longer rely on a row-based, scale-up, costly data warehouse to meet most needs, quite often we've placed data in the architecture in disparate places.

With data virtualization, the business intelligence can be provided much more rapidly because we are removing data integration. However, the performance may suffer a bit from a physically coupled data set.

If you look at 100 BI requirements, perhaps 15 will be interesting in 6 months. There are 85 requirements that you will fulfill that serve a short-term need. This does not diminish their importance. They still need to be done, but it does mean they may not need to be quite as ruggedized. One study by the Data Warehousing Institute[2] showed the average change to a data warehouse takes 7–8 weeks.

---

[2] Business Intelligence Benchmark Report 2011.

At Pfizer, cross–system BI requirements will be met initially through data virtualization in the manner I described. After a certain number of months, if the requirement is still interesting, they will then look into whether the performance is adequate or should be improved with data integration.

You need data virtualization capability in the shop in order to compete like this. Talk about being agile (Chapter 16)! If you accept the premise of a heterogeneous environment, data virtualization is fundamental. I would also put cloud computing (Chapter 13), data governance, and enterprise data integration capabilities in that category.

> Stand-alone virtualization tools have a very broad base of data stores they can connect to, while embedded virtualization in tools providing capabilities like data storage, data integration, and business intelligence tend to provide virtualization to other technology within their close-knit set of products, such as partners. You need to decide if independent virtualization capabilities are necessary. The more capabilities, the more flexibility and ability to deliver you will have.

Simplifying Data Access

Abstracting complexity away from the end user is part of self-service business intelligence, discussed in Chapter 15. Virtual structures are as accessible as physical structures when you have crossed the bridge to data virtualization. While the physical structures and data sources, so are virtual structures. This increases the data access possibilities exponentially.

Data virtualization also abstracts the many ways and APIs to access some of the islands of data in the organization such as ODBC, JDBC, JMS, Java Packages, SAP MAPIs, etc. Security can also be managed at the virtual layer using LDAP or Active Directory.

> ## When Not to do Data Virtualization
> There may be some reports that perform well enough and are run infrequently enough that it may make sense to virtualize them, but there is another perspective and that is auditability. Going back to a point in time for a virtual (multi-platform) query is difficult to impossible. It requires that all systems involved keep all historical data consistently. I would not trust my Sarbanes–Oxley compliance reports or reports that produce numbers for Wall Street to data virtualization. Physicalize those.

> Similarly, when performance is king, as I've mentioned, you'll achieve better performance with physical instantiation of all the data into a single data set. Mobile applications in particular (covered in Chapter 15) need advanced levels of performance, given the nature of their use.
>
> While I have somewhat championed data virtualization in this chapter, these guidelines should serve as some guardrails as to its limitations. It is not a cure-all for bad design, bad data quality, or bad architecture.

Combining with Historical Data

At some point in time, in systems without temperature sensitivity that automatically route data to colder, cheaper storage, many will purposefully route older data to slower mediums. The best case for this data is that it is never needed again. However, it is kept around because it might be needed. If that time comes, the data is often joined with data in hot storage to form an analysis of a longer stretch of data than what is available there. The cross–platform query capabilities of data virtualization are ideal for such a case.

This also serves as a proxy for the "odd query" for data across mediums. This is the query that you do not want to spend a lot of time optimizing because it is infrequent. The users know that and understand.

ACTION PLAN

- Determine existing data virtualization capabilities within current tools
- Acquire the needed data virtualization capabilities if necessary
- Utilize data virtualization to solve business intelligence requirements requiring cross-system data
- Analyze your process for data platform selection to ensure proper fit of data to platform for most (never all) of its uses

REFERENCE

Davis, J.R., Eve, R., 2011. Data Virtualization: Going Beyond Traditional Data Integration to Achieve Business Agility. Nine Five One Press, U.S., p. 176.

CHAPTER TEN

Operational Big Data: Key-Value, Document, and Column Stores: Hash Tables Reborn

In the mid-2000s, several new-economy Silicon Valley companies were facing data challenges at a scale beyond those of the largest companies in the world. Knowing the exploitation of that data was the essence of their business, and knowing the existing relational technology would be too expensive to scale—if it even could scale to their needs—many companies independently set out to build their own solutions. The commonalities were many among the internal solutions and most reached a similar conclusion about the SQL/relational/transactionally-sound marketplace—it did not have a place in the solutions.

As discussions took place across the Valley, a Meetup was formed to share findings and advance the solutions. That Meetup needed a name and a poll occurred. Jumping on this fact that the solutions had all ignored or banished SQL, the name of "No SQL" was decided on and a movement was begun.

Initially, the movement's players were adamant that the solutions would rule the enterprise,[1] but as initial outreach of this storyline was met with disinterest from enterprises, the "No" came to be known as "NO" as in "Not Only SQL." I cannot say I like the "No" or "NO" as a label. Any time you name a space something that it is not, it creates issues. Walls form in prospects that believe you are anti- all the software they have in house—and that you will not integrate with it. Prospects also will think of all of the capabilities they have with SQL and believe the "no" solution will not do any of them. This is not true, although there are definitely some capabilities that are not present. Also, the interfaces are so quickly coming close to SQL that it would difficult to imagine the space being named NoSQL today. I'm here to help you with the industry, not create new terms, so let's talk about NoSQL.

---

[1] This mindset still exists out there

Before we leave semantics, there is a very important term that is very related here. Big data is synonymous with the NoSQL movement because these Valley companies that originated the movement had "big" data challenges. If the data were "small," they would not have created the space and would have just used relational technology. The literature uses NoSQL and big data synonymously, but really the big data is the data being stored in the NoSQL solutions and what the NoSQL solutions store is, by definition, big data.

This is almost, but not completely, true. Graph databases, discussed in Chapter 12, provide extremely valuable functionality for relationship data—and that data need not be "big."

WHEN TO YES NOSQL

You may be looking for the quantifiable definition of big data. Again, it's the workload threshold when relational no longer makes sense—given your unique situation. It's hard to imagine that under a certain single-digit number of terabytes—unless you have a specialized single-use workload that matches well with the pros of NoSQL and minimizes the cons of NoSQL—that it makes sense.

Many will say that big data/NoSQL[2] is a Valley phenomenon and your company does not have a need to get out of the SQL comfort zone. Not so fast. NoSQL enterprise deployments are mostly for net new applications in the business—exactly those applications that have big data needs. It's a perfect storm of need and solution.

Why Big Data Now?
There are a few trends bringing us into the era of big data.
* Storing Data is Cheaper than Ever
  Companies increasingly are feeling liberated by less expensive means for extending the competitive advantages of data exploitation into more voluminous data: clicks, weblogs, and sensor reads of small movements. Factors that are triggering the liberation include past-decade exponential decreases in the cost of all computing resources and an explosion in network bandwidth.

[2]I'll call it NoSQL from this point forward in the book

- Sensor Networks

    Most people don't think of their cell phone as part of a "sensor network." However, their increased ubiquity and web connection are impossible to ignore as data collection mechanisms. One day, we may be able to opt in to contributing our air quality, air pressure, noise level, or other "around me" data to our favorite companies we do business with. Today, we contribute our location, web clicks, and application usage. Cell phones are examples of the growing sensor network, with great adoption in supply chains.

- History Data

    Many get into data warehousing entertaining the notion that they will remove data as it becomes old and less useful—perhaps at the 3-year point and perhaps to something as cheap and inaccessible as tape. However, as long as the warehouse is successful enough to make it to that point, the users are inevitably interested in ALL the data and need fast access to all the data. Tiering some of it to lower-cost storage, perhaps some of the big data options—like Hadoop, for example—is possible, but inaccessible, slow tape is not.

- Syndicated Data

    The third-party data marketplace, discussed in Chapter 7, is booming and dispensing data to the enterprise in many cases as much as, or more than, the enterprise generates internally. This potentially significant additional avenue of interesting data can dramatically expand enterprise information.

    Not all of these trends directly correlate to the need for a NoSQL solution, but they are making enterprise information "bigger."

- Ability to Utilize the Data

    Just as successful data warehouses result in user need for all the data they've ever seen in the data warehouse, likewise high-end analysts (sometimes referred to as Data Scientists) are finding business uses for all data—including data types they have never utilized before—which usually falls into the big data category.

There are many other aspects of NoSQL that define its best workload other than cheaply storing a large amount of data.

Achieving high availability cheaply would be another important consideration.

Data model flexibility, defined later in the chapter, would be another good indicator that NoSQL is a correct categorization for the workload.

In general, it is the sensor data, full webclick data, social data, and related offshoots, such as those attributed later in the chapter to certain of the models, that make for the best fit in NoSQL stores. Enterprises have mostly been force-fitting snapshots and summaries of this data into relational databases for years and now it's time to realize the full potential of big data.

NOSQL ATTRIBUTES
Open Source

Most of the NoSQL movement has an open source component. While most of the players in enterprise decision making are familiar with open source, it remains an enigma in the enterprise itself. Certainly, being able to take on software with an open source origin in the enterprise is a requirement for taking on NoSQL and, consequently, a requirement for success in IT today.

Many NoSQL companies have high triage with the open source software they support, in addition to the support and related software they add on to that software. Still, the support model is not the same as enterprise "closed source" software. An enterprise can make it passable, even excellent, with effort, but will likely find a new set of challenges given the abstraction of support from software owner (the "community" in open source) to a third-party company.

Data Models

NoSQL solutions do not require, or accept, a preplanned data model whereby every record has the same fields and each field of a table has to be accounted for in each record. Though there can be strong similarities[3] from record to record, there is no "carryover" from one record to the next and each field is encoded with JavaScript Object Notation.

(JSON) or Extensible Markup Language (XML)—according to the solution's architecture. A record may look like:

- Book: "War and Peace": Author: "Tolstoy"

This is what is meant by unstructured data- Data of varying forms loaded without a set schema.[4]

---

[3] the level of similarities will help drive a NoSQL categorization decision—the column store being particularly good for a high level of similarity from record to record

[4] "Give me your tired, your poor, Your huddled masses…" of data

> ## Abstact Programming in Relational Databases
> Many attempt to simulate the data model flexibility in a relational system through abstract programming techniques.
> 1. "Dummy" fields like COLUMN32, COLUMN33, COLUMN34, etc. that are usually large VARCHARs and accept the variable fields of the record
> 2. Heavy use of subtypes and supertypes in tables
> 3. Storing column names in fields
> 4. "Code tables" with a code numbering system that spans codes
>
> These techniques may make sense in relational systems if other factors are involved that make relational best for the workload. However, if a flexible data model is a primary consideration in the workload, consider a NoSQL solution.

Scale Out

It has long been a truism that to achieve scaling to higher and higher levels,[5] it is less expensive to do it with smaller machines than larger machines. In the early days of computing, as systems began to tackle scaling challenges with larger machines, the costs took off exponentially. Machines were getting much more complex. A 10-terabyte system could cost not 10 times a 1-terabyte system, but nearly 100 times. If you wanted to store 10 terabytes, you paid the price. This is scale up.

NoSQL solutions found a way to multiply that 1-terabyte system 10 times: at 10, not 100, times the cost. The key is the divide and conquer, exemplified by MapReduce, discussed later in the chapter. By dividing the programming across a single data set spread over many machines, NoSQL is able to keep the costs down and the scale up (I mean out!).

The following sections are also traits of NoSQL solutions that are dissimilar to relational databases. However, their nature could differ from NoSQL solution to NoSQL solution. I advise you get your solution into the right category first, then make sure the solution adheres to the characteristics of these traits that are needed by the application.

Sharding

Sharding is a partitioning pattern for the NoSQL age. It's a partitioning pattern that places each partition in potentially separate servers—potentially

---

[5] I'll use levels of data as an example, but scale also refers to the computing done with the data

all over the world. This scale out works well for supporting people all over the world accessing different parts of the data set with performance. If you are taking an order for someone in Dallas, for example, that order can be placed in the Southwest U.S. data center.

A shard is managed by a single server. Based on the replication schema, the shard is most likely replicated twice on other shards. Shards can be set up to split automatically when they get too large or they can be more directed. Auto-sharding takes a load off of the programming, which would otherwise not only have to manage the placement of data, but also the application code's data retrieval.

Consistency

ACID (see box) is essential for guaranteeing 100% accuracy when you have many rows spanning many tables in a single operation. The operation should succeed or fail completely and concurrent operations are isolated so partial updates do not commit.

Most NoSQL solutions do not have full ACID compliance like a relational system does. This inhibits its abilities to do critical financial transactions. Each record will be consistent, but transactions are usually guaranteed to be "eventually consistent" which means changes to data could be staggered to the queries of that data for a short period of time.[6] Some queries are looking at "old" data while some may be looking at "new" data. Consider the business model behind the application to determine the fit of the consistency model of the solution. The trade-off for this downside is improved performance and scalability.

No vendor has been able to articulate the risk of the lack of full ACID compliance of a NoSQL solution. Also, I know of no one who has experienced some sort of transaction, and hence business, failure as a result of overcommitting transactions to NoSQL. Still, it IS theoretically possible that a transaction could fail unless full ACID is guaranteed and, for that reason, critical money matters should not be committed (pun) to NoSQL.

---

[6] frequently within tens or hundreds of milliseconds

> ## What is ACID?
> - Atomicity – full transactions pass or fail
> - Consistency – database in valid state after each transaction
> - Isolation – transactions do not interfere with one another
> - Durability – transactions remain committed no matter what (e.g., crashes)

Though the most important component of ACID is atomicity, the more complex component is consistency. Consistency may be tunable by the NoSQL database administrator. By tuning the replication factor and the number of nodes that will respond to a write, the system can follow a more or less "write tolerant" profile. Not only writes, but also the replication, can have this inconsistency window. The effect of replication on consistency can be profound. Consistency can often be tuned on a session basis.

Commodity Components

"Commodity" is a class of hardware and does not refer to your old Tandy 1000s, TRS-80s, Burroughs B2500s, and the like. It is, however, an unspecialized level of computer, somewhere in the mid–single digit thousands of dollars that can be effectively used in NoSQL systems. The scale-out architectures are built to utilize this class of computer.

MapReduce

The idea of MapReduce has been around quite a while. Lisp Systems had the same concept decades ago, but Google effectively revived it as the primary access mechanism for NoSQL systems. The idea is to take a large problem and divide it into locally processed subproblems. As much of a query as possible will be processed in the node where the data is held. That part of the query is the same for all nodes. That is called the Map function. The same homogeneity is true for the Reduce step, which follows the Map step and the movement of the data within the nodes to where it can be effectively utilized.

Both the Map and the Reduce are programmed using Java (primarily). While many organizations have attempted to marginalize or eliminate programming from their shop for internal "system integrator" types who can install and customize software, with NoSQL, you need to bring those skills back!

Sample MapReduce Code: Find Out How Many Times Each Account Was Accessed In The Last 10 Years[7]

```
map(key, value)
    {
    // key = byte offset in log file
    // value = a line in the log file
    if (value is an account access audit log)
    {
    account number = parse account from value
    output key = account number, value = 1
    }
    }
    reduce(key, list of values)
    {
    // key = account number
    // list of values {1,1,1,1......}
    for each value
    count = count + value
    output key, count
    }
```

[7] Credit: Java Code Geeks http://www.javacodegeeks.com/2011/05/mapreduce-soft-introduction.html

Each Map and Reduce also specifies how much parallelism across the nodes, potentially thousands, there will be. MapReduce runs in batch and always completely scans all the nodes, being careful to avoid reading the same data twice due to the replication. The replication factor is usually three, so figure the scans are reading slightly more than 1/3 of the nodes with every MapReduce job.

Cloud Computing

While not required, the volume and unpredicatability of the data selected for NoSQL make the cloud an ideal place to store the data. Cloud computing will be covered in detail in Chapter 13, but breaking into NoSQL often means breaking into the cloud—two ideals worth achieving.

Up until now, I have not even mentioned the 800-pound gorilla of big data that is Hadoop. I will defer that to its own chapter 11, but all of the NoSQL origins, common attributes (open source, model flexibility, scale out), and those attributes that differ from solution-to-solution—but most likely differ from a relational solution (sharding, concurrency, JSON, MapReduce, HTTP Based Interface)—are present with Hadoop.

While a Hadoop file system is the gathering place for transactional big data for analytics and long-term storage, numerous other forms of NoSQL are available and one or more could be needed for a modern enterprise although for quite different purposes. These NoSQL stores primarily serve an operational purpose—with some exceptions noted. They support the new class of "webscale" applications in which usage, and hence data, can expand and contract quickly like an accordion.

Much non-Hadoop NoSQL support is heavily intertwined with the application and supported by the application teams and not necessarily the information management team. It might be tempting to select from these solutions without giving much "enterprise" thought to the matter. However, an organization with one webscale application usually could soon have several. It would be advantageous to have skills around a single multipurpose NoSQL solution, especially within a NoSQL categorization.

All of the categories later in the chapter support thousands of concurrent users needing their data in real time—a pulsating system of vibrant activity made possible with recent advances in internet and network capabilities. Without NoSQL, many of the applications in use today that were "invented" in the last decade would not have access to the data they need to exist.

NOSQL CATEGORIZATION

These categories of NoSQL beyond Hadoop are mostly key-value in nature. They do not have proper data models, but instead store the key (column name in relational vernacular) followed by the value for each column. We refer to this as a "hash table." Like Hadoop, this allows each record ("aggregate") to be constituted quite differently, although often the records will be similar. As we'll see, the similar/dissimilar nature of the records is a determining factor for the category.

The emerging NoSQL space has had many entrants and quite possibly quite a few more already than can survive for very long. It is important to categorize the vendor products as I have done here. In technical spaces in this book with durations of at least a few years—namely all but the NoSQL group—the analyst and user communities have pushed vendors into appropriate categories.

NoSQL has not hit this threshold yet, so the vendors still largely abhor the categorizations in an attempt to keep all their cards on the table. Even Hadoop distributors can be loose in their marketing, bleeding over into these other NoSQL categories. Look beyond vendor self-categorization. It's usually less that the product defines a supercategory or defies categorization than it is that the product fits one category.

These are good categories to learn about so you can make the proper categorization, put the wares into the correct category, and make the correct selection.

> **Value Per Capita**
> The "value per capita" (e.g., value per terabyte) of big data is going to be less than the value per capita of data that is stored in a relational solution. Nonetheless, if that value exceeds the cost, that data should come under management as well. Over time, we may find that the aggregate value of managed big data exceeds that of relational data.

KEY-VALUE STORES

Key-value stores have little to no understanding of the value part of the key. It is simply a blob, keyed by a unique identifier which serves a "primary key" function. This key is used for get, put, and delete. You can also search inside the value, although the performance may be suboptimal. The application consuming the record will need to know what to do with the blob/value.

Key-value stores are effectively used for keeping track of everything related to the new class of web, console, and mobile applications that are run simultaneously by thousands of users, sometimes sharing sessions, as in games. The value is the full session or game–state information with every session having a unique key.

Key-value stores are also used for shopping carts, which can persist over time. User Preferences are similar from a data perspective and stored in key-value stores. Both seek to create availability of the information from any platform (browser, console) at any time.

Many companies are taking advantage of NoSQL stores to personalize and optimize the web experience for their current web presence(s) without regard to the product the company produces.

The commonality in these uses is that the primary use of this data is the need to look up the full session information at once and to do so by a single key.

Key-value stores are prominent today, but with a few additional features they can become a document store or a column store. As a result, this may be a dying category. Some products have migrated categories. However, when records are simple and lack strong commonality of look, a key-value store may be all you need.

Keep in mind document stores and column stores are also key-value in the sense of how data is stored—as a hash table. However, their additional capabilities earn them a separate categorization. These capabilities, discussed in their respective sections later in the chapter, also highlight some of the workloads you do not want to use a key-value store for: those involving relationships amongst data, complexity of data, or the need to operate on multiple keys/records at once.

DOCUMENT STORES

Document stores are specialized key-value stores. As the name implies, the model is particularly good at storing and retrieving actual documents. However, the term "document" actually is the document store's term for the record.

Documents can be nested. In addition to key-value stores, document stores add the ability to store lists, arrays, and sets. It is an excellent model when fields have a variable number of values (e.g., addresses, "likes," phone numbers, cart items) according to the record. Of course, that number could be zero for a given record. And unlike key-value stores, the value part of the field can be queried. The entire document/record does not need to be retrieved by the key. It is good when more granular data than full records is required.

Document stores tend to be excellent for logging online events of different types when those events can have varying characteristics. They work well as pseudo content management systems that support website content. Due to the ability to manipulate at a granular level, document stores are good for real-time analytics that change dynamically, which the application can take advantage of immediately.

COLUMN STORES

A column store is a key-value store that is conceptually similar to the column database I talked about in Chapter 5, whereby each column's values (or set grouping of columns) are stored independently. Column stores somewhat defy the idea that each record is independently crafted with no forced schema. In column stores, defined column families

MUST exist in each record. This makes the column store ideal for semi-structured data in which there is some commonality, as well as differences, record to record. Column families would be comprised of columns that have similar access characteristics.

Column stores are ideal for application state information across a side variety of users. Blogging, with its similar columns for each record, are also semi-structured, as are some content management systems.

Given the "modeling" (still light by relational standards!) that is done for column stores, for data that is still relatively unknown, column stores may prove to be too restrictive. However, when the query pattern is by subsets of the entire record, the added ability to create column families makes the column store attractive.

NoSQL in the Enterprise

The NoSQL community can rapidly accelerate its progress in the enterprise by:

1. Making *reasonable* recommendations for NoSQL use
2. Communicating and educating
3. Documenting the expected record profiles (data model)
4. Helping IT with their agile, cloud, and open source knowledge and adoption – nonstarters for NoSQL projects
5. Developing ROI around their projects
6. Developing strategies early for integration with enterprise data
7. Making NoSQL ware easier to use and fitting it into frameworks
8. Tackling softer issues of these projects, like program and data governance

 # NOSQL SOLUTION CHECKLIST

Characteristic	Importance/Ideal	Rating	Comments
Model (KV, Doc, Col)			
Open Source			
Data Models			
Scale Out			
Sharding			
Consistency			
Commodity Components			
MapReduce			
Cloud Computing			

ACTION PLAN

- As a prerequisite to NoSQL deployments, get comfortable with open source technology, develop a cloud computing strategy (Chapter 13), and adopt an agile methodology (Chapter 16)
- Determine what you are doing with available sensor, social, and webclick data today; possibly more could be captured with NoSQL adoption
- Likewise, determine if any source data is not being captured because of limitations of relational technology
- When web applications are being considered or are in development, put the appropriate NoSQL technology (key-value, document, or column store) on the proverbial table

CHAPTER ELEVEN

Analytical Big Data: Hadoop: Analytics at Scale

A new technology has emerged in recent years that was formed initially in 2006 for the needs of the Silicon Valley data elite. The companies had data needs that far surpassed any budget for DBMS out there. The scale was another order of magnitude away from the target for the DBMS. The timing of the scale was not certain, given the variability of the data. It's not like Google wanted to be bound by calculations that enterprises go through like "by next year at this time, we'll have 3 petabytes so let's build to that." They didn't know.

Hadoop was originally developed by Doug Cutting who named it after his son's toy elephant. Today, Yahoo is the biggest contributor to the Hadoop open source project. Eventually, the code for Hadoop (written in Java) was placed into open source, where it remains today. However, today as enterprises far and wide have found use for Hadoop, there are several value-added companies like HortonWorks and Cloudera that support a particular version of Hadoop. Some have developed some supporting code that is under closed source. Most enterprises find working with one of these vendors to be more functional than pure open source (Apache) Hadoop, but you could go to http://hadoop.apache.org/ and download Hadoop yourself.

Hadoop is quickly making its way down from the largest web-data companies through the Fortune 1000 and will see adoption in certain upper midmarket companies in the next 5 to 10 years.

The description here of Hadoop applies to all the variations of Hadoop. I have found nothing in the variations that would sway a decision about whether a workload belongs in Hadoop or not. Choosing the particular "distribution" of Hadoop is analogous to choosing the DBMS or business intelligence tool. Getting enterprises appropriately into the platforms is the focus of this book. As this applies to Hadoop, there is some information you need to know.

BIG DATA FOR HADOOP

Although I get calls frequently during budget season (usually 3rd quarter) about replacing some of the large DBMS budgets with Hadoop, seldom does that make sense.[1] Hadoop will replace little of what we now have (and plan to or could have in the future) in our data warehouses. Sometimes the rationale for thinking about Hadoop is a belief that the multiple terabytes in the data warehouse constitutes "big data" and Hadoop is for big data analytics.

I explained in the previous chapter what big data is. You should now know that there is ample data out there that is not in the data warehouse, nor should be, that constitutes the big data of Hadoop. It will ultimately be more data by volume than what is in the data warehouse—maybe petabytes. It's the data we've willfully chosen to ignore to date. Hadoop specializes in unstructured and semi-structured data such as web logs.

Data updates are not possible yet in Hadoop, but appends are.

Most shops have struggled with the management of this data and have chosen to ignore unstructured and semi-structured data because it's less valuable (per capita) than the alphanumeric data of the standard data warehouse. Given the cost to store this data in a data warehouse, and the lower ROI per byte, it's mostly only summaries or critical pieces that get managed. Those who once stored this data in their data warehouse have either become disenchanted with the cost or have abandoned the idea for other reasons. But there is value in detailed big data.

HADOOP DEFINED

Hadoop is an important part of the NoSQL movement that usually refers to a couple of open source products—Hadoop Distributed File System (HDFS), a derivative of the Google File System, and MapReduce—although the Hadoop family of products extends into a product set that keeps growing. HDFS and MapReduce were codesigned, developed, and deployed to work together.

Hadoop adoption—a bit of a hurdle to clear—is worth it when the unstructured data to be managed (considering history, too) reaches dozens of terabytes. Hadoop scales very well, and relatively cheaply, so you do not have to accurately predict the data size at the outset. Summaries of the analytics are likely valuable to the data warehouse, so interaction will occur.

[1] Except for the occasional use of Hadoop as cold storage for older, seldom-accessed data in DBMS

The user consumption profile is not necessarily a high number of user queries with a modern business intelligence tool (although many access capabilities are being built for those tools to Hadoop) and the ideal resting state of that model is not dimensional. These are data-intensive workloads, and the schemas are more of an afterthought. Fields can vary from record to record. From one record to another, it is not necessary to use even one common field, although Hadoop is best for a small number of large files that tend to have some repeatability from record to record.

Record sets that have at least a few similar fields tend to be called "semi-structured," as opposed to unstructured. Web logs are a good example of semi-structured. Either way, Hadoop is the store for these "nonstructured" sets of big data. Let's dissect Hadoop by first looking at its file system.

HADOOP DISTRIBUTED FILE SYSTEM

HDFS is based on a paper Google published about their Google File System. It runs on a large cluster of commodity-class nodes (computers). Whenever a node is placed in the IP range as specified by a "NameNode," one of the necessary Java virtual machines, it becomes game for data storage in the file system and will report a heartbeat henceforth to the NameNode.

Upon adding the node, HDFS may rebalance the nodes by redistributing data to that node.

Sharding can be utilized to spread the data set to nodes across data centers, potentially all across the world, if required.

A rack is a collection of nodes, usually dozens, that are physically stored close together and are connected to a network switch. A Hadoop cluster is a collection of racks. This could include up to thousands of machines.

There is one NameNode in the cluster (and a backup NameNode). This NameNode should receive priority in terms of hardware specification, especially memory. Its metadata—about the file system—should be kept totally in memory. NameNode failures, while not catastrophic (since there is the backup NameNode), do require manual intervention today. DataNodes are slaves to the NameNode.

Hadoop data is not considered sequenced and is in 64 MB (usually), 128 MB, or 256 MB block sizes (although records can span blocks) and is replicated a number of times (3 is default) to ensure redundancy (instead of RAID or mirroring). Each block is stored as a separate file in the local file system (e.g. NTFS). Hadoop programmers have no control over how HDFS works and where it chooses to place the files. The nodes that contain data, which is well over 99% of them, are called DataNodes.

It must be noted that NoSQL systems other than Hadoop use HDFS or something very similar. Sometimes it's called HDFS even if it's different. Some call their offerings a "version of Hadoop" even if it's not HDFS. On behalf of the industry, I apologize.

Where the three replicas are placed is entirely up to the NameNode. The objectives are load balancing, fast access, and fault tolerance. Assuming three is the number of replicas, the first copy is written to the node creating the file. The second is written to a separate node within the same rack. This minimizes cross-network traffic. The third copy is written to a node in a different rack to support the possibility of switch failure. Nodes are fully functional computers so they handle these writes to their local disk.

Cloud computing (Chapter 13) is a great fit for Hadoop. In the cloud, a Hadoop cluster can be set up quickly. The elasticity on demand feature of cloud computing is essential when you get into Hadoop-scale data.

MAPREDUCE FOR HADOOP

MapReduce was discussed in the previous chapter and is the means of data access in Hadoop. I'll say a few things here about its applicability to Hadoop for bringing the processing to the data, instead of the other way around.

All data is processed in the local node in the map operation. Map and reduce are successive steps in processing a query, with the reducer doing the processing on the output of all of the mappers after that output is transferred across the network. Multiple reduce tasks for a query is not typical.

For example, a query may want a sum by a group, such as sales by region. Hadoop MapReduce can execute this query on each node in the map step. The map step is always the *same* code executed on *each* node. The degree of parallelism is also fungible. For example, if you say 10 levels of parallelism and there are 200 nodes, the map will spawn itself 10 times to be executed across 20 nodes each. MapReduce jobs are full scan and considered batch in nature. It will eventually complete the parallel scan and have 10 sums for each group. The sum across these collective groups then needs to be done. This subsequent step to the map is a reduce step. Nodes are selected for the reduce by the HDFS and the sums are distributed to those nodes for the overall summations. Again, the degree of parallelism is selected. This time, there will only be as many nodes as the degree of parallelism in the map step.

Both the map and reduce are written in a programming language, usually Java. The jobs need only be written once, identified as a map or reduce, and will spawn according to the parallelism.

This is the embodiment of taking a large problem, breaking it into smaller problems, performing the same function on all of the smaller problems, and, finally, combining the output for a result set.

Due to the redundant blocks, MapReduce needs a way to determine which blocks to read. If it read each block in the cluster, it would read three times as many as necessary! The JobTracker node manages this activity. It also waves the jobs through as they come to the cluster. There is not much in the way of native workload management, but this is improving through the supporting tools listed below. When the job is ready, off it goes into the cluster. The JobTracker is smart about directing traffic in terms of the blocks it selects for reading for the queries.

The JobTracker schedules the Map tasks and Reduce tasks on "TaskTracker" nodes and monitors for any failing tasks that need to be rescheduled on a different TaskTracker. To achieve the parallelism for your map and reduce tasks, there are many TaskTrackers in a Hadoop cluster. TaskTrackers utilize Java Virtual Machines to run the map and reduce tasks.

Queries will scan the entire file, such as ones that come up with the "you might likes" in social media that recur to many levels deep in web logs to return the best fit. Like a data warehouse, Hadoop is read-only, but is even more restrictive in this regard.

FAILOVER

Unlike DBMS scale-up architectures, Hadoop clusters, with commodity-class nodes, will experience more failure. The replication makes up for this. Hadoop replicates the data across different computers, so that if one goes down, the data are processed on one of the replicated computers. Since there is (usually) 3x replication, there are more than enough copies in the cluster to accommodate failover. HDFS will actually not repair nodes right away. It does it in a "batch" fashion.

Like a lot of things in Hadoop, the fault tolerance is simple, efficient, and effective.

Failure types:
  Disk errors and failures
  DataNode failures
  Switch/Rack failures
  NameNode (and backup NameNode) failures
  Datacenter failures

HADOOP DISTRIBUTIONS

There are several variations of the Hadoop footprint, with more undoubtedly to come. Prominently, there is open source Apache/Yahoo, for which support is also available through Hortonworks and Cloudera, currently independent companies. EMC, IBM with BigInsights, and the Oracle Big Data Appliance also come with training and support. So while Hadoop footprints are supported, one must choose a distribution for something they most likely have no live experience with.

Distributions are guaranteed to have components that work together between HDFS, MapReduce, and all of the supporting tools. They are tested and packaged. With the many components, this is not trivial added value.

SUPPORTING TOOLS

Hive and Pig are part of distributions and are good for accessing HDFS data with some abstraction from MapReduce. Both tools generate MapReduce jobs, since that is the way to access Hadoop data.

Facebook and Yahoo reached a different conclusion about the value of declarative languages like SQL from Google. Facebook produced an SQL-like language called Hive and Yahoo! produced a slightly more procedural language (with steps) called Pig. Hive and Pig queries get compiled into a sequence of MapReduce jobs.

There is also column store HBase that works with Hadoop. It is used in the Bing search engine. Its primary use is to hold web page crawler results. It mainly keeps track of URLs (keys), critical web page content (columns), and time stamps for that page (what changed version control). It provides a simple interface to the distributed data that allows incremental processing. HBase can be accessed by Hive, Pig, and MapReduce.

There is also Sqoop, a package for MapReduce jobs to move data between HDFS and DBMS.

Here are some other components:

Mahout – machine learning

Ambari – reports what is happening in the cluster

Cascading – high level tool that translates to MapReduce (like Pig and Hive)

Oozie – workflow coordination management; you define when you want MapReduce jobs to run, trigger when data is available, and launch MapReduce jobs

Flume – streaming data into Hadoop for MapReduce, Pig, Hive

Protobuf, Avrò, Thrift – for serialization

HCatalog – Hadoop metadata; increasingly, business intelligence and ETL tools will be able to access HDFS through HCatalog

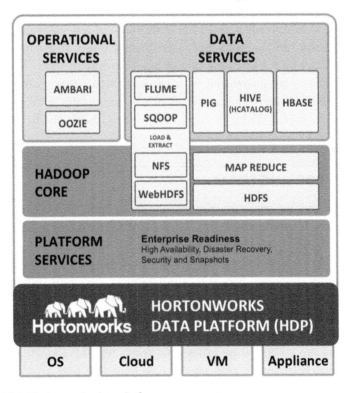

Figure 11.1 Hortonworks data platform components.

HADOOP CHALLENGES

Hadoop implementation is complex. It's a programming orientation as opposed to a tool orientation. Programmers rule this world and have often isolated themselves from the internal "system integrators" who deploy tools. These groups often do more than build. They analyze, which is also different from information management in the database-only years.

The server requirements are immense, mostly because we are dealing with large amounts of data that require many servers. However, for many organizations, these commodity servers are harder to implement than enterprise-class servers. Many organizations are used to vertical scaling and not to supporting "server farms."

The divide between the Hadoop implementation team and management is more pronounced as well. It is interesting that at the same time that hands-off software-as-a-service is reaching new heights in organizations, this labor-intensive, brute-force approach antithesis to software-as-a-service is making sense in those same organizations.

Large vendors are responding to the Hadoop challenge in two ways—and usually both ways at once. One way is the "join them" approach, where the vendor announces Hadoop distributions in addition to continuing full support of their current wares for "big data," many of which are now extending their capabilities to an unprecedented scale. Others incorporate Hadoop-like capabilities as a hedge against Hadoop and a reinforcement of their road map, much of which began prior to Hadoop availability.

HADOOP IS NOT

Hadoop is not good for processing transactions or for other forms of random access. It is best for large scans. It is also not good for processing lots of small files or intensive calculations with little data.

We have become accustomed to real-time interactivity with data, but use cases for Hadoop must fall into batch processing. Hadoop also does not support indexing or an SQL interface—not yet, anyway. And it's not strictly ACID-compliant, so you would not manage transactions there.

Types of Data Fit for Hadoop
- Sensor Data – Pulsing sensor readers provide this granular activity data
- Clickstream Data – Detailed website visitor clicks and movements
- Social Data – Internet-áccumulated data entered
- Server Logs – Logs interesting for diagnosing processes in detail
- Smart Grid Data – Data to optimize production and prevent grid failure
- Electronic Medical Records – Data for supporting clinical trials and optimize
- Video and Pictures – High-storage and dense objects which generates patterns
- Unstructured Text – Accumulated text which generates patterns
- Geolocation Data – Location data
- Any high volume data that outscales DBMS value
- Very "cold" enterprise data with no immediate or known utility

This is very interesting as I know of no one who has tried to do something in Hadoop and failed because it did not have ACID compliance. This is mainly due to good workload selection, but the fact that transactions *could* fail—even if you're not doing them in Hadoop—gives a lot of technology leaders pause about using Hadoop. Due to its *eventual* consistency, it *could* have less-than-full transactions committed—a big no-no for transactions. Again, this is theoretically possible given the eventual consistency. I have not been able to create a failure or know of anyone who has. Furthermore, nobody has been able to articulate the risk—in mathematical terms—that you are undertaking with transactions in Hadoop. I am NOT advocating doing transactions in Hadoop, just pointing this out.

Are these knockout factors for Hadoop? I don't believe so. In my work, large unstructured batch data seems to have a cost-effective and functional home only in Hadoop. Any Hadoop will at most coexist within the enterprise with its less expensive per capita server farms processing large amounts of unstructured data, passing some of it to relational systems with broader capabilities, while those relational systems continue to do the bulk of an enterprise's processing, especially of structured data.

The advancement of the Hadoop tool set will obviate some of the Hadoop limitations. Hadoop should begin to be matched up against the real challenges of the enterprise now.

SUMMARY

In summary, Hadoop changes how we view the data warehouse. Shops with unstructured data in the dozens of terabytes and more—even to petabytes—may adopt Hadoop. The data warehouse no longer needs to be the biggest data store, although it will still process the most queries and handle most of the alphanumeric workload. The data warehouse will continue to process ad hoc, interactive queries. However, analytic queries that require unstructured and semi-structured data will move to Hadoop.

ACTION PLAN

1. Develop an understanding of the full costs of Hadoop.
2. Ease into Hadoop. Download open source Hadoop.
3. Pick a problem to solve. Don't start with egregious problems and petabytes of data. As you are learning the technology and its bounds, as well as the organization's interests, deliver time-blocked projects with business impact.
   a. Move any unstructured analytical data you may be storing in a DBMS to Hadoop
   b. Explore the organization's need for unstructured analytical data it may not be storing, for potentially storing in Hadoop
4. Extend governance to Hadoop data and implementations.
5. Consider technical integration points with the "legacy" environment.

CHAPTER TWELVE

Graph Databases: When Relationships are the Data

There is at least one application of NoSQL technology to a workload that makes sense even when the data is not necessarily massive. DBMS models used to have a primary focus on the relationships amongst data. Interestingly, and perhaps ironically, the focus of the relationships in RDBMSs is generally between discrete things that were broken apart (normalized) in order to be stored using the relational model. In contrast, relationships in graph databases are used to relate just about anything, including different types of relationships for like things (people to people, etc.).

Precursors to the relational model—such as hierarchical and later, network—models stored data with meticulous navigational information. Relational turned out to be a better fit for the heterogeneous workloads for the data and took care of the relationship aspects with referential integrity. Further, relational is a good fit for types of data that are inherently tabular and static, such as invoices, order forms, and general ledgers.

Eventually, the modern demands have grown to require the model to fit the workload more closely to drive performance, and graph databases have emerged to, once again, emphasize data relationships. The types of data that people care to monetize these days is more complex and interconnected (i.e., real-world systems, which are by their nature highly interconnected) vs. form data as one has in accounting, which for decades was perhaps the major driver behind much of the IT innovation that occurred when RDBMSs came to the fore in the 80s and 90s. Workloads, likewise, have emerged that emphasize relationships. When relationships are the important aspect to the data, graph databases shine. The data does not have to be petabytes, terabytes, or hundreds of gigabytes, even, for the graph database to provide significant performance benefits over other database technologies.

"Graph" is probably not the most operable term for this class of databases, as it conjures up an image of something with fixed rows and columns and predictable connections (e.g., graph paper). The old term of network may be better, but—regardless—it's a fit when relationships matter most.

The data itself can be homogenous, such as all people and their relationships as in a "social graph." For this, you can think of Twitter and how we're all connected. Fast checks of how many degrees off we are from each other or list pulls of all those a certain number of degrees apart, are workloads that would be nested table self-joins in relational databases— not a fast path query. Those queries can be enormously complex. DBMS optimizers' interpretations can be quiet variable and costly as well.

Here's example SQL for finding the author's friends-of-friends:

Select pf1.person as person, pf3.person as friend_of
From personfriend pf1 inner join person
On pf1.person = person.person
Inner join personfriend pf2
On pf1.friend = pf2.person
Inner join personfriend pf3
On pf2.friend = pf3.person
Where pf1.person = 'William McKnight' and pf3.person < > 'William McKnight'

●●●——

Graph databases also yield very consistent execution times that are not dependent on the number of nodes in the graph, whereas relational database performance will decrease as the total size of the data set increases.

Other NoSQL models are even less of a fit for the relationship workload due to their lack of support for relationships in the model itself. Their cost is exacerbated with deep levels of a graph. Think friends of friends of friends of friends. Dealing with these exponentially expanding limitations in other NoSQL models will cause you to accept functionality limitations. Many of these systems try to maintain the appearance of graph-like processing, but inevitably it's done in batches and is not real-time.

Why You Need to Do a Friends of Friends Query

One reason is to make accurate recommendations. According to James Fowler, a social scientist specializing in social networks, cooperation, political participation, and genopolitics, one's 2nd and 3rd degree connections exert a great influence on our lives, which is very interesting as this includes people we may not know! The second is that the hops can be between different types of things (i.e. heterogeneous hops). I recently met with a Neo4j customer whose typical queries are of degree eight. The highest I've heard of is a customer who is benchmarking queries with a degree of over 200.

I'll get to the nature of the structure of the graph database that facilitates these kinds of queries later. Graph databases are more specialized in their best fit than most of the other structures here, so I will spend some more time describing their best workload, the relationship workload.

●●●

A node representing the author might look like CREATE Author = {firstname: 'William', lastname: 'McKnight'}. This node is assigned to the identifier Author. This node is now available. The Author identifier is used later in code to attach relationships to the node. For example, the clause CREATE (author)[:WROTE{date:2014}]-> (Information Management)" creates a WROTE relationship from Author to the book Information Management, the one you now hold in your hand or ereader.

Social graphs may be the most obvious example of a graph database use, but it is actually not the most dominant. Many graph implementations use heterogeneous nodes, as in Figure 12.2. If you can visualize it as a graph, it may make sense to be in a graph database. Graph analysis is relevant in many industries and in companies large and small. Consider some of these examples:

- The previously mentioned social networking. Sites like Facebook, Twitter, LinkedIn, etc. are all interested in network-generated social connections. These connections are the lifeblood of their concepts and their navigation must be done in real-time (under 200 ms) because this information is used for everything from online recommendations to user login to parcel routing, and is used thousands of times a day.
- Flight path analysis. Consider airlines visualizing all of the flights in and out of various airports and overlaying the route graph with costs, distances, and other factors to determine where to put new routes.
- Financial traffic analysis. What are the popular routes between institutions, accounts, and people of money flow? Where is fraud and money laundering about to happen?
- Transportation network analysis. Where do packages and, therefore, vehicles (all kinds) need to maneuver to optimally deliver, given the constraints of time and money?
- Continuing the idea of "connections," telecommunications companies sit on some very interesting connections—connections that call or text one another, with frequency, time, and location dimensions.

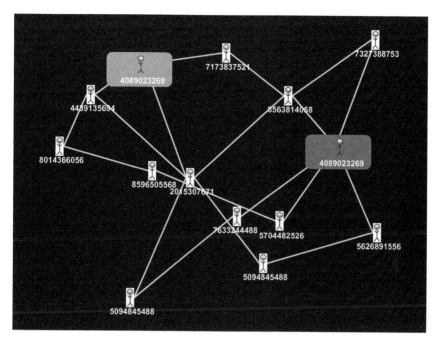

Figure 12.1 Graph database showing who called whom.

- Website navigation analysis. How do visitors navigate the site? What pages do they traverse and in what order? This knowledge leads to better website design. The internet itself is a network of connected pages, which makes storage of any navigation of your own site, or other sites, fit for a graph database.
- Crime and terrorism is seldom done in a vacuum. How people and organizations are related around these topics is of interest to government agencies and companies concerned with fraud like financial systems companies.
- Propensity to purchase. When this is needed in order to make a fast next-best-offer based on precalculated metrics, graph databases shine. They can be used to find out who is similar to the person and who has a similar history of purchases and market baskets.

There's also recommendation engines, geospatial analysis, product catalogs, biotechnology applications, genealogy research, and linguistic data that is relationship-based.

Taking a broad view of relationships, you can see that relationships are everywhere. Once you start thinking this way, the possibilities for graph

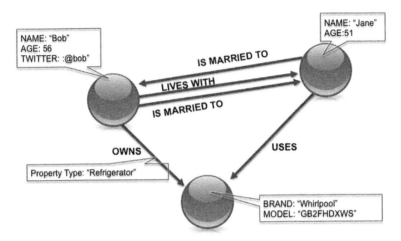

Figure 12.2 A graph with heterogeneous nodes.

databases expand. Relationships are the foundation for graph databases. Graph databases are optimized around data relationships.

Graph database benefits are exacerbated when there is this relationship type of workload for more nodes. A leading graph database server, Neo4J, accepts up to tens of billions of nodes, tens of billions of relationships, and tens of billions of properties (and will soon be lifting these limits).

An example with only nodes representing "friends" finds a large cluster of people connected to all of their friends (connected to their friends, etc.). This inability to definitively draw lines around which very few relationships cross (think of the Oprah effect[1] on the Twitter graph) makes sharding difficult.

Should a graph exceed the capacity of a cluster then graphs can be still spread across database instances if the *application* builds in sharding logic. Sharding involves the use of a synthetic identifier to join records across database instances at the application level. How well this will perform depends very much on the shape of the graph.

Some graphs will lend themselves to this.

Of course, not all graphs have such convenient boundaries. If your graph is large enough that it needs to be broken up and no natural boundaries exist, then the approach you would use is much the same as

[1] The Oprah effect is an expression referring to the effect that an appearance on The Oprah Winfrey Show, or an endorsement by Oprah Winfrey, can have on a business. Because the show reaches millions of viewers each week, a recommendation from Oprah can have a significant and often unexpected influence for a new or struggling business. Source: Investopedia

one would use with a NOSQL store like MongoDB—create synthetic keys and relate records via the application layer using those keys plus some application-level resolution algorithm.

Like other NoSQL databases, graph databases also excel at high availability. With features like master-slave replication, automatic failover with master reelection, and clustering with remote read-only slave nodes for disaster recovery.

●●● ──

Queries run fastest when the portions of the graph needed to satisfy them reside in main memory. A single graph database instance today can hold many billions of nodes, relationships, and properties; some graphs, therefore, will just be too big to fit into the main memory of a single instance. Ways of optimizing in such scenarios have evolved. For example, Neo Technology's "cache sharding" relies on the natural cache affinity that results when one load balances across a cluster in a consistent manner. Here, queries are routed to instances in such a way that each instance ends up with a different part of the graph in memory, allowing queries to find their data in memory more often than not.

TERMS

Graph – A collection of nodes and relationships

Node – The object of interest in a graph. A node contains a set of (name, value) pairs. There can be multiple types of nodes in a single graph. Nodes are essentially the records in a graph database.

Traversal – The navigation of a graph to determine connections, degrees of separation, and shortest paths.

Properties – Attributes of a node or relationship. Relationships – Connections between nodes with a direction. Relationships have properties as well.

Queries – Traversals of the graph.

Paths – development; as well as that between development of an application, and the ability for that application to perisist dataan nsid Routes between nodes, including traversed relationships

While not applicable in every situation, these general guidelines will help you to choose when to use nodes and when to use relationships:

- Use nodes to represent entities—that is, the things that are of interest to you in your domain.
- Use relationships to express the connections between entities and establish semantic context for each entity, thereby structuring the domain.

- Use node properties to represent entity attributes, plus any necessary entity metadata, such as timestamps, version numbers, etc.
- Use relationship properties to express the strength, weight, or quality of a relationship, plus any necessary relationship metadata, such as timestamps, version numbers, etc.

STRUCTURE

Like nodes, relationships can have properties such as the age or relationship (public, private) of the relationship represented.

Neo4j, for example, stores graph data spread across a number of store files. Each store file contains the data for a specific part of the graph (e.g. nodes, relationships, properties). The division of storage responsibilities—particularly the separation of graph structure from property data—exists for high performance graph traversals even if it means the user's view of their graph and the actual records on disk are structurally dissimilar.

The structure does not accept SQL. For example, Cypher is the language used with Neo4J. It contains the commands necessary to get nodes, traverse nodes, and return values. It's SQL-like for traversing relationships to find values or the existence of values. One very cool feature is to limit the "degrees" that are searched in a query. More about Cypher in the next section.

As alluded to in the examples above, graph traversal can focus on a specific path, finding an optimal path, or the importance ("centrality") of a path.

In specific path analysis, the graph database will move from out of a node in all directions looking for the relationship. Until it is found, the pattern repeats until the relationship is found or the edge of the graph is reached.

With optimal path analysis, the shortest path is found between two nodes. This yields the level of connectedness—the closer the nodes in the graph, the closer the relationship.

Modeling for a graph database is "whiteboard friendly." By this, I mean it is how a user would model the problem on a whiteboard. There is close affinity between the logical and physical graph models, which closes various project gaps, including those between requirements analysis, design, and the start of development; as well as that between development of an application and the ability for that application to persist (write/ store) data. Relational modeling requires more transformations from the real world to its implementations. There is also no concept of the denormalization technique done to relational models, which impacts relatability in order to improve performance.

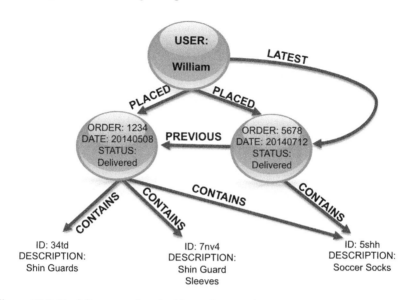

Figure 12.3 Modeling a user's order history in a graph.

CENTRALITY ANALYSIS

Finally, there is centrality analysis. Various measures of the centrality of a node have been defined in graph theory, which underlies the graph database. The higher the measure, the more "important" the node. Here are some different ways to measure centrality:

- *Degree centrality:* This is simply the number of edges of the edge. The more edges, relatively speaking within the graph, the more important the node. The nodes with higher edges (i.e., the more "important" customers, products, etc.) typically looks like a "hub" of activity if you were to visualize the graph.
- *Closeness centrality:* This measure is the inverse of the sum of all shortest paths to other vertices. Closeness can be regarded as a measure of how fast it will take to spread information to all other nodes. If a node has strong closeness centrality, it is in a position, with its relationships, to spread information quickly. These people (if nodes are people in the graph) can be important influencers of the network.

- *Betweenness centrality:* As an indicator of how many paths a node is on, its betweenness centrality demonstrates how many paths it is a part of, which represent that node's ability to make connections to other groups in the graph.
- *Eigenvector centrality:* Finally, there is eigenvector centrality, which assigns scores to all nodes in the network that indicate the importance of a node in a graph. Scores are assigned based on the principle that high-scoring nodes contribute more to the score than equal connections to low-scoring vertices.

LinkedIn's Graph Database

LinkedIn has a neat feature which shows you a visualization of your LinkedIn network.

See http://inmaps.linkedinlabs.com/. This is an example of the power of a graph database.

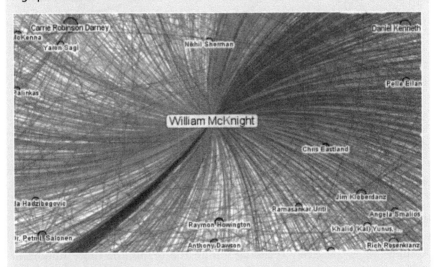

Figure 12.4 Central portion of the author's LinkedIn "InMap."

CYPHER, A GRAPH DATABASE LANGUAGE

To demonstrate some of the characteristics of a language used with a graph database, I'll look at Cypher, the language for Neo4J—one of the leading graph databases.

Cypher is a pattern-matching query language. It uses declarative grammar with clauses, which is like SQL. It has aggregation, ordering, and limits and you can create, read, update, or delete. Most queries follow a pattern in which an index is used simply to find a starting node (or nodes), and the remainder of the traversal uses a combination of pointer chasing and pattern matching to search the data store.

Here is an example of Cypher commands to get a node, traverse a node and return all the friends of friends.

//get node with id 0
start a = node(0) return a
//traverse from node 1
start a = node(1) match(a)→(b) return b
//return friends of friends
start a = node(1) match(a)—()—(c) return c

Here is an example in Cypher for pulling a list of "friend of friends":
start n = node:People(name = 'William McKnight')
match (n)—()—(foaf) return foaf

●●●————————————————————————————————————

Other Examples of graph database servers are InfiniteGraph, AllegroGraph RDFStore, STIG from Tagged, and VertexDB.

GRAPH DATABASE MODELS

Neo4J is considered a property graph, which is a "directed, labeled, attributed multigraph" that exposes three building blocks: nodes, typed relationships, and key-value properties on both nodes and relationships. Another graph model is RDF Triples, which is a URI-centered subject-predicate-object triples as pioneered by the semantic web movement. Finally there's HyperGraph, which is a generalized graph in which a relationship can connect an arbitrary number of nodes (compared to the more common binary graph models).

Hypergraph is a generalized graph model in which a relationship (called a hyper-edge) can connect any number of nodes. More specifically, while the property graph model permits a relationship to have a single start and end node, the hypergraph model allows any number of nodes at a relationship's start and end.

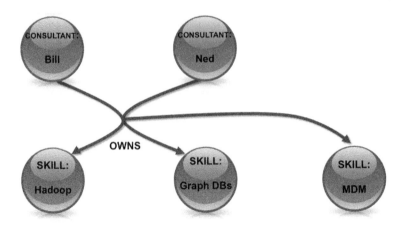

Figure 12.5 A simple (directed) hypergraph.

Property graphs are the most pragmatic, giving properties to nodes to make them easier to work with.

Since I am choosing only timeless material for this book and these distinctions could change, it doesn't make sense to go too deeply into the differences in graph types, especially when I see the "best of" each being a part of all graph databases in the future. Graph databases are, however, very stable in their architecture. *Graph databases* is sufficient as a category for purposes of allocating workload.

Those relationship-oriented workloads—described above plus their offshoots—find multiple benefits of being on a graph database as opposed to a relational database. These benefits include:

1. Query execution speed
2. Reduced application development cycles for developing the queries
3. Extensibility, scalability, and failover

As with other data stores described in this book, if you are after the power of performance, it behooves you to place, or move, workloads into the data stores that, primarily, deliver that performance. Performance is a powerful motivator for using the graph database for the relationship workload.

ACTION PLAN

• Analyze workloads to see if what is really important in them is relationships.

- Analyze workloads to see if performance issues are predominantly related to navigating relationships.
- Consider the workloads discussed in this chapter, and ones that are similar, for graph databases.

CHAPTER THIRTEEN

Cloud Computing: On-Demand Elasticity

Everyone is talking about the cloud—and for good reason. Nothing will change the way IT operates like cloud computing. Those of us who have been deploying applications for a long time are used to being able to, at some point, perform maintenance and upgrades, or perhaps simply view, our physical servers. Those days are passing us by.

Server management is one of those functions that is not considered part of the core competencies in developing applications. It is increasingly being delivered by service level to applications, including information management applications that need servers to function, which is most of them.

Service levels will include things like up time, response time, data size, tiered performance levels, level of willing risk (vs. cost), resource management needs, etc. Though these may seem to constitute a quite reasonable range of the needs of an information management application, if there is any temptation to turn over platform selection to the cloud provider, let me dissuade you from that type of thinking. The information management owner needs to make those decisions, the decisions that this book is geared toward supporting.

The Changing Nature of IT

IT was once determined to be best fit in an organization as a central organization, providing all of the technical services that the organization requires. As of this writing, it still is in many organizations. However, many other organizations are taking a more balanced approach with IT. There is still a central IT, but there is latitude for distributed IT organizations (most likely not in name, but in function). Wherever the technical roles reside is what I mean when I reference "IT."

DEFINING CLOUD COMPUTING

So what is "the cloud" and how does it fit into this discussion of turning server management over to service levels? The cloud is perhaps the most nebulous (or nebula ☺) term in technology. At one end of the spectrum (spectra ☺), the cloud is erroneously used as a term to simply mean the Systems Administration group no longer wants to allow you to see your server due to difficulties with security access, the questions that the visits raise, or as a means of emphasizing the split in responsibilities between Systems Administration and the application teams. This can be referred to as a "private cloud." However, I will give some criteria later that I think a true private cloud adheres to—some good functionality that provides true value to an organization.

At the other end of the spectrum, you have established public clouds like Amazon Web Services, Softlayer (an IBM Company), Rackspace, GoGrid, etc. that provide exhaustive services that go beyond the basic cloud criteria I will give you later.

The best definition for cloud computing I've found is the one by the U.S. National Institute for Standards and Technology (NIST).

It defines cloud computing as "*a model for enabling convenient, on-demand network access to a shared pool of configurable computing resources (e.g., networks, servers, storage, applications, and services) that can be rapidly provisioned and released with minimal management effort or service provider interaction.*"[1] NIST defines the 5 characteristics of cloud computing as:

- On-Demand and Self-Service
- Broad Network Access
- Resource Pooling
- Rapid Elasticity
- Measured Service

On-demand and self-service disintermediate IT and others from an application owner and her ability to provision servers. Broad Network Access means access to a wide variety of modern platforms—much more than one could get on its own. Resource Pooling is gaining the benefits of economies of scale. Rapid Elasticity is the "accordion effect" of resources growing and shrinking seamlessly as needs dictate. Measured Services refers to the reporting infrastructure of the cloud provider, providing detailed reports to you on usage.

We are all consumers of cloud services, whether we refer to it as such or not. We might use a version of Microsoft Office in the cloud (starting with Version 365), DropBox or Google Docs for file sharing, iCloud from Apple, etc. Public email services are cloud based. Many organizations use one of the first pieces of software ready for the enterprise from the cloud: salesforce.com (whose phone number is 1-800-*NO-SOFTWARE*). Salesforce.com software is for contact management and many see this as an enterprise function that

---

[1] http://csrc.nist.gov/publications/nistpubs/800-145/SP800-145.pdf

can be easily isolated. However, the idea of offloading not only the servers referenced above, but also the software (installation, maintenance, upgrades, etc.), is catching on in many enterprise domains, including all of the ones related to information management—data storage, data integration, data access, etc.

●●●
_____

The cloud is a metaphor for the internet and telephone networks.
_____

You are completely hamstrung these days selecting information management software and hardware if you patently rule out the cloud option. In many areas, the cloud options are the rule, not the exception. You may end up with pockets of software, hardware, and data in many clouds—private and public—and your new dominant role in IT is to choose and integrate wisely.[2]

Information management is a frequent leading domain in bringing the cloud strategy to an organization or taking the strategy to new levels. The cloud is essential for the information manager to understand, which I why I must talk about it in this book on information management.

Moving into the Cloud[3]

The most elaborate public cloud that I've visited is the Switch SuperNAP in Las Vegas (www.switchlv.com). This is where companies like eBay, Google, DreamWorks, Sony, Cisco, Pixar, Joyent, HP, Vmware, Nirvanix, and many others call home for their server infrastructure.

The SuperNAP is the world's most efficient, high-density data center in the world. It is (currently) 2,200,000 square feet of data center space for 520,000 square feet of operational data space with 500 megavolt amperes (MVA) of power capacity, 567 MVA of generator capacity, and 294 MVA of Uninterruptible Power Supply.

The highly redundant systems and service levels for on-call power delivery would seem to make it the last building to lose any power if the worst were to happen. Electrical power inside Switch facilities is delivered on System + System design so each primary and failover system is completely separated from the other. The fault-tolerant power design enables Switch to deliver 100 percent power uptime to its customers. As needed, the SuperNAP can be power self-sufficient with its inclusion of up to fifty 2.8 megawatt diesel generators onsite for a total of 140 megawatts of generator capacity.

The cooling system is a work of art itself. With 202,000 tons of cooling, it has 22,000,000 CFM (cubic feet per minute) of airflow. Depending on weather

_____

[2] Since it interacts with so many systems, master data management is a challenging choice for the cloud.

[3] Reference: http://mike2.openmethodology.org/wiki/Going_into_the_premier_cloud

conditions, the system chooses which of the four ways it has at its disposal to cool. Each customer has a private secure caged area called t-scif™ that enables higher power and cooling densities per cabinet than any other data center in the world.

They also believe the location supports, rather than competes with the cooling system. As hot as Las Vegas is understood to be, 70% of the time the temperature is 72 degrees or less (i.e., nighttime). The temperatures are consistent. As well, Las Vegas is one of the few places without a real threat of natural disasters like floods, hurricanes, and earthquakes.

The cleanliness rivals the clean rooms where chips are made. Our guards said the physical aspects were the most important element to security. The armed escort guards at either end of our group certainly attested to that.

And in those over 31,000 cabinets reside the data that is supported by this infrastructure and made available in many forms, including collocation, connectivity, and cloud computing. This is data that many of us interact with daily. SuperNAP clients are built on data and have huge downsides if transactions are not collected, hospital records are compromised, or television content fails.

The SuperNAP is simply unattainable infrastructure for a company to build for themselves. Yet, it reflects the pseudo-requirements that I see all of the time. This is what it takes to provide true "99.9999%" availability. I was impressed with the decision making process across so many factors that the designers must have gone through.

Similarly, many companies are looking to build their own private clouds and evaluate public cloud providers and will need to determine their requirements. The SuperNAP sets the bar. While designs and public clouds state high availability, greenness, efficiency, security, performance (eBay's numbers are outstanding), and elasticity, it's the infrastructure that delivers.

Figure 13.1 The switch SuperNAP.

BENEFITS OF THE CLOUD

Why are companies embracing arms-length arrangements with hardware and software? Why do CIOs repeatedly tell me that they need to get more and more of their databases to the cloud in short order?

One of the important categories is cost. You pay only for what you use and you pay a third party for the resources on a periodic basis—usually monthly. The cloud lowers in-house staff requirements as well as the physical requirements for a proper data center, which brings costs down for power, floor storage, and network systems—not the core competency for most organizations.

More importantly, the costs are treated, for tax purposes, as operational costs (OPEX), whereas internally managed systems are usually capital expenses (CAPEX) and written off over time. The whole OPEX vs. CAPEX debate is outside the scope of this book, but there is no doubt that the cloud is an enabler of OPEX, which is highly favorable to the CFO.

VMS found that "The overall 5-year TCO savings for SAP systems running on cloud range between 15% and 22% over identical systems that are deployed on-premises or outsourced. You pay only for what you use. When using cloud, you turn infrastructure costs from being capital expenses into variable operational costs."[4]

The other area of major benefit of the cloud is in deployment or provisioning speed. It should be ready when you are. When I've laid out timetables for projects recently, I've had CIOs tell me the cloud provisioning is so fast, it's to the point of being uncomfortable. They are used to lining up resources, support, and project details during the time it usually takes to provision the hardware, but here I am saying the *software* is ready for us to use this week.

Certainly, the fast provisioning of the cloud will require some getting used to!

The cloud also obviates that whole guesstimation process that projects go through early on to try to determine how much space and resources they are going to need. This has seldom turned out to be within 25% of accuracy. Either the project does extraordinarily well, in which case it exceeds its estimates, or it bombs and dramatically underutilizes the estimates.

[4]http://www.vms.net/content/e457/e458/e1707/items1711/VMS_EN_TCO_Study_AWS_with_CWI_EXTRACT_205_ger.pdf

●●●

I have done provisioning only to have it padded (by 2X) by one level of management ("just in case") only to be padded (by another 2X) by another level of management (also "just in case"). Disk costs keep coming down, but this approach is overkill.

With its dynamic provisioning capability, cloud resources are going to expand and contract according to need, like an accordion. I still recommend the projects go through a rough estimating exercise, if only to ensure a proper platform selection. However, with the cloud, companies will not be saddled with unused resources. Also, if worse comes to worst for a project (or company), it will be a major benefit in deprovisioning to be in the cloud.

Certainly with the data sizes involved in big data (Chapters 10 and 11), the cloud makes the utmost of sense—large, fast-growing amounts of non-sensitive data for which it is extremely difficult to estimate its ultimate size.

CHALLENGES WITH THE CLOUD

Although the arguments are slowing down, security remains the biggest challenge to using the cloud for information management. After all, you are turning data over to a third party.

●●●

Early cloud deployments fueled the security concern by commingling data, even for large companies, in the same servers. Now, "single tenant" (no commingling) and "multi-tenant" (commingling) is a decision point in a cloud deployment. Initially, single tenant came with prohibitive extra cost, but, as it has become the norm, additional costs for single tenant are minimal or nothing.

Performance of a prospective information management cloud deployment must be tested—load, query, failover, etc. Performance can be an issue, although recent tests are showing performance for most tasks equivalent to or better than in-house deployments.

The multiple clouds that inevitably will support an organization cause issues as well, which is a large reason for thinking about the company's cloud strategy from a holistic, top-down perspective as well as tactically project-by-project. If cloud platforms need data from each other, how will they get it? While it's usually possible (worst case: cloud 1 to on-premises, on-premises to cloud 2), the performance could be an issue. Again, test performance across the clouds you are considering.

Moving to the cloud can also feel like buying a franchise business. You can change some things, but not the big things.[5] Standards could be different. While you're seldom locked into a cloud contract for long, should you wish to bring the data back in-house or go with another cloud provider, that process is effort-laden and time-intensive. I believe the industry will evolve to have more portability, much like the telecommunications industry mandates allowing portability of phone numbers in 1996 and 2003.

Availability can be an issue that may dictate which applications are put in the cloud. Reliability and performance are also variable around the world, depending on the country's networking infrastructure, among other things.

Finally, there are regulatory requirements that prohibit some cross-country storage of data. This affects the smaller European countries more than companies based in the U.S. The Patriot Act,[6] for example, prohibits Canadian companies from using US clouds.

Cloud Availability

Availability can be an issue as well with the cloud. Not all cloud providers are like the SuperNAP. Amazon Web Services (AWS) famously provides 99.95% availability, far less than the 99.9999% availability that many applications aspire to. While this may seem like a lower class of service (and occasionally it's not met), CIOs are rationalizing that the aspiration of 99.9999% availability is simply that—an aspiration that is not realized by most in-house implementations.

When, occasionally, AWS has gone down,[7] the anticipated exodus from AWS did not happen. Instead, companies opted in to more failover from AWS!

●●●

Image naming, server clocks, and time zones become a real challenge with the cloud if not managed well.

While I've found public clouds usually measure up to the cloud criteria above quite well, private clouds need to evolve to meet the criteria. With captive private clouds (i.e., your former System Administration group), old habits die hard. All of the characteristics could be compromised unless

[5] Especially with public cloud. Some captive private clouds are malleable
[6] Full content of the Patriot Act: http://www.gpo.gov/fdsys/pkg/PLAW-107publ56/html/PLAW-107publ56.htm
[7] AWS credits 5% of the fee for every 30 minutes of downtime

there is a corresponding mindset change (very challenging, see the chapter on Organizational Change Management). Usually the last characteristic to accomplish for a private cloud is sufficiently broad network access. By starting out with in-house servers, there is seldom broad network access. A private cloud must provide inventory and choice to its customers. Servers to accommodate most of the data stores referenced in this book, including Hadoop, need to be made available.

Cloud Provider Agreements

There are many "line item" costs in a cloud provider agreement. Several have to do with the level of knowledge the provider will give to you about the servers provisioned for your needs. Even though you may not know what to do with them immediately, it is best to pay for all of these insights. You're already saving dollars. Pay the nickels for this insight.

CLOUD DEPLOYMENT MODELS

Throughout this chapter, I have referenced the public and private cloud options. I will now say more about them and the other major options you have in developing a cloud strategy for information management.

The public versus private cloud is the dimension with the most leverage in a cloud strategy. The direction of public or private will absolutely influence not only every cloud decision, but perhaps every software decision the company will make henceforth. Public clouds are made available to a broad audience—not just your company. Public clouds are in the *business* of providing virtual infrastructure to companies. While providers certainly compete on features and functions, they are much more homogeneous than private clouds.

The term "private cloud" is highly abused as it can be used to refer to, as I've said, the System Administration group creating some space and distance for itself. However, I've seen just as many excellent and quickly matured private clouds that offer all of the 5 characteristics of cloud computing.

Sometimes they get so good that they become a cloud that can be shared with other companies. At some point in that progression, the cloud can become a "hybrid" cloud. Hybrid can also be used to refer to a company's cloud strategy of utilizing BOTH public and private clouds. This I see as an inevitable path for information management.

The Path to Hybrid Cloud

Enterprises need to evolve their current IT infrastructure to become more "cloud-like"—to become a better internal service provider to the lines of business and departments and to provide greater agility and responsiveness to business needs, higher quality of service in terms of latency and availability, lower costs, and higher utilization.

The first step that many enterprises are taking is to move to a virtualized environment—a private cloud that moves from a dedicated, rigid, physical structure for each application to a virtual environment with shared services, dynamic provisioning, and standardized configurations or appliances.

This is a self-service and pay-per-use environment. A user goes to the employee portal, signs in, makes a request for a virtual machine(s) with a certain amount of CPU, memory and disk, picks a VM image for database or middleware, then clicks "submit." If that employee's role and entitlements allow him or her to have that amount of IT resource, then it gets provisioned without an IT person being involved. If not, perhaps his or her request gets routed to his or her manager and/or IT for workflow approval.

Ultimately, the best arrangement will be "hybrid clouds," combining both a private cloud or clouds and multiple public clouds.

The second major dimension of emphasis in a cloud strategy is what category of service the cloud is expected to provide. There are three categories:

- Software-as-a-Service (SaaS),[8]
- Platform-as-a-Service (PaaS), and
- Infrastructure-as-a-Service (IaaS).

IaaS is the lowest category of service and gives you access to servers, storage, and networking over the internet. Amazon famously provides this level of service. A way to look at IaaS is that it's just VMs in the cloud. Adding the middleware and operating system to the servers, storage, and networking is PaaS—platform-as-a-service.

SaaS are the cloud services we are all familiar with such as email, collaboration tools, productivity tools, Google applications, etc. The previously mentioned salesforce.com is also SaaS. SaaS provides "everything"—just sign up and use the software today. There is limited customization, especially at the server level. There is limited to no visibility at the server level because it is controlled by the software provider. Usually

---

[8] yes, the "aa" is lowercase in the acronyms

these providers are aware that an enterprise runs on much more software than theirs and provides APIs to access your data should you want to distribute it to other servers and clouds.

As individuals, many of us consume SaaS applications on the cloud daily, such as Google Apps, DropBox, and iCloud. Perhaps the most prominent enterprise package using a SaaS model is salesforce.com.

The third dimension of cloud computing is also addressing "what" you are putting on the cloud and this is where the possibilities have become numerous. Take a data warehouse, with its sourcing/integration/transformation, data storage, and data access layers, broadly speaking. Any one, two, or three of these can be placed into the cloud, irrespective of the others. Many are starting with the database and working "out" to the data access layer.

The voyage into the cloud can begin from any of the combinations of the dimensions: public/private, IaaS/PaaS/IaaS, and the chosen layer. It should be a mindful evolution to multiple forms—with lessons learned and absorbed along the way—that the organization can take through the worthwhile journey into the cloud.

A Look at Platform-as-a-Service

Of the services choices, PaaS provides the strong combination of commoditized services and application flexibility that makes sense for many information management needs. In many ways, it essentially becomes the organization's operating system.

PaaS must provide support for the programming languages to be used by the developers. Microsoft.NET, Java, PERL, Python, and RUBY developers will need those capabilities in the PaaS APIs they program to. Many shops will need multiple programming languages available.

The nice stress remover from the organization with PaaS has to do with the fact that it talks to its infrastructure through APIs. These programmatic calls between layers remove much of the integration challenges in the components between the hardware and the operating system, such as networks, ports, and disks. Resource allocation to the application layer is also handled by PaaS, focusing the organization on its application development, not its infrastructure.

For example, Jaspersoft, a prominent business intelligence software company, has ported its commercial open source business intelligence solutions to OpenShift Flex by Red Hat, which uses Amazon Elastic Compute Cloud (EC2)[9] for the IaaS layer and supports a wide range of development languages. The suite now provides convenient tools to work with the applications and platforms

[9] https://aws.amazon/ec2

there, MongoDB (a document store, see Chapter 10) being notable due to its integration into OpenShift as well as being previously supported by Jaspersoft.

Some PaaS characteristics to keep in mind are whether it is closed or open source, public or private cloud, and what programming languages are supported.

Although most PaaS solutions are public cloud, some are designed such that they could be taken to the private cloud. Here again, the larger enterprise cloud decision will affect the PaaS solution choice. The important aspect of this decision is the proximity and interaction with the other cloud(s) of the organization. The inevitable integration with the on-premises systems must be considered, especially the performance of the integration. Smart deployments take this into account and collocate systems with a high degree of sharing needed.

Open Source software is often associated with the cloud, since you are often looking for inexpensive software when you're looking for a quick-provisioned, inexpensive environment. For an excellent treatment of Open Source in Business Intelligence, see "Using Open Source Platforms for Business Intelligence: Avoid Pitfalls and Maximize ROI," by Lyndsay Wise.

INFORMATION MANAGEMENT IN THE CLOUD

Any or all layers of an information management stack can be placed in the cloud. Consider a data warehouse stack of data platform, data integration, and data access. Most will opt to put the data platform in the cloud first, whereas others would start with the software running in the cloud, following the data.

Among cloud benefits, the largest ones for information management are:
- Flexibility to scale computing resources
- Ability to shorten implementation windows
- Reduced cost
- Testing, development, sandboxing environments
- Geographic scalability

In order to keep one project on-time and on-budget, we decided to build the environment in the cloud. In five days, we were able to build the complete BI landscape in the cloud, load the data, schedule the ongoing loads, and build the data access layer. In a traditional on-premises hosting environment, this landscape would have taken weeks to months to create.

ACTION PLAN

- Inventory organizationally proximate uses of the cloud today
- Understand your company's abilities and aspirations for a private cloud
- Evaluate public cloud providers and understand their services for your information management needs
- During the next information management software contract review, mentally compute what it would look like to deploy that software in the cloud
- Determine your desired SaaS, IaaS, and PaaS footprint profile

CHAPTER FOURTEEN

An Elegant Architecture Where Information Flows

If you've been reading from the beginning, by now I have reviewed with you all of the major data platforms, permutations, and workloads. Now it's time to put it all together.

THE STARTING POINT

On the operational side, where business transactions are forged, there has been less change in recent years than on the analytical side. Most organizations look at the line between operational and analytical systems as fairly hard and fast, and resources are allocated as such. Most operational systems are based on relational databases. The pattern over time that the operational systems, especially the more common Enterprise Resource Planning (ERP) programs like SAP, go through are:

1. We provide all of the reporting you would ever need right out of the ERP system.
2. When concurrency issues happen with that database and customers begin to need to do extensive development of reports, a separate database—akin to a data mart or warehouse—is built, where you can also try to integrate other data.
3. Concurrency issues are obviated and some additional structures are commingled with the operational database; integration with other data is still challenging.
4. A balance is struck between operational/ERP reporting and post-operational data mart/warehouse reporting, with the latter being used primarily for analytical reporting, for form-fit reporting, and when data integration is necessary.

Though it's hard to generalize, many information environments will be loosely centered around one, or a few, data warehouses. See Figure 14.1. These will feed data marts a subset of the data in the warehouse for more specific consumption profiles. There will also be numerous marts that sit in isolation. No environment is without these inelegant structures due to

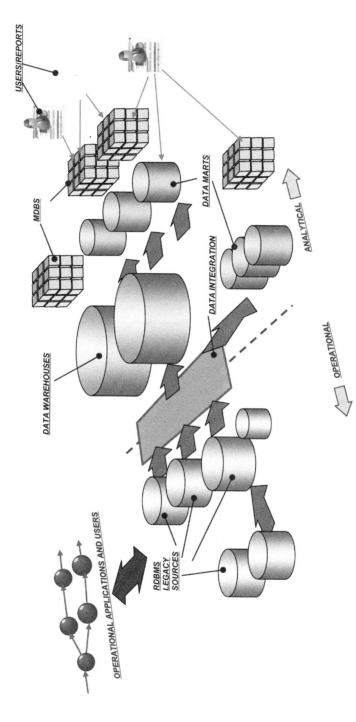

Figure 14.1 Desired information architecture through 2013.

reasons of expediency and difficulty integrating with IT structures like the data warehouse.

Many of today's environments can have many multidimensional/cube structures. Like data marts, these can be fed from operational sources, data marts, or data warehouses. Similar to how marts are structured, analytical cubes should be fed from the data warehouse, where data is (theoretically) guaranteed to be "clean" (see Chapter 4) according to corporate governance and to otherwise conform to standard.

Where cubes have been introduced into an organization, they can expand their footprint, either in number or size. I have provided a Data Warehouse Rescue Service to many organizations over the years and one of the main reasons is abuse of the cube idea. While organizations are largely moving forward into new areas regardless of the current situation, there are a couple of areas of projects that are well worth pursuing:

1. Data Warehouse Consolidation
2. Cube Consolidation

PLENTY OF WORK TO BE DONE

The architecture to move organizations into the next couple of decades is the No-Reference architecture. See Figure 14.2. It is labeled No-Reference to distinguish it from hard-and-fast references. It is a guideline as to where things belong relatively and what technologies are viable, but there are many permutations, especially when it comes to the data warehouse/marts/appliances and Hadoop section.

I have been giving Action Plans in each chapter. The summation of all of the action plans leads you to the No-Reference Architecture.

I have added many items to the Starting Point architecture. You will notice the new functions placed into both the "post-operational" (right-hand) side of the line and the operational side. There is no one-size-fits-all when it comes to optimizing the important information asset.

●●●

The hard line between an operational side and an analytical side to information management is blurring. Reporting, analytics, and integration are needed everywhere. The skills owned by the analytical-side people are now needed everywhere in the organization. As a result, Information Management is a discipline being led more by those with analytics, data quality, and integration skills than operational/ERP skills.

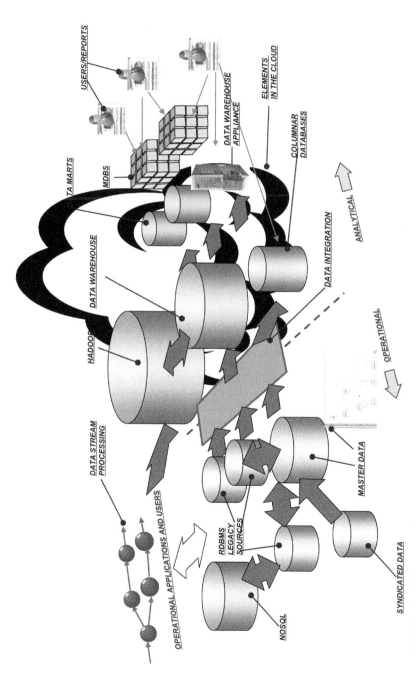

Figure 14.2 The No-Reference information architecture.

Master Data Management is worthwhile just about everywhere. The biggest problem with MDM is the long, strange justification cycle. Getting cooperation from different departments about value proposition is always a challenge. To keep Figure 14.2 from looking like spaghetti, it shows MDM feeding some of the other operational systems, but in reality MDM will eventually feed just about ALL of the systems in the No-Reference Architecture. This could be, as described in Chapter 7, feeding structures fit for working with that system, or it could be allowing access to the data in the master hub. Regardless, the data that gets IN to the MDM hub will be considered clean and governed, which may necessitate a workflow process with manual involvement from multiple constituencies—which is what the workflow icon in Figure 14.2 references.

Continuing around the architecture for its additions from the Starting Point, there is syndicated data. Syndicated data is not a new data store. It is a new class of data being brought into the architecture. I show it in the MDM hub, as discussed in the chapter on MDM.

In the Operational Applications and Users area, we are now doing more business intelligence in the form of Data Stream Processing, discussed in Chapter 8. High velocity data with real-time needs can be processed before it is optionally stored with Data Stream Processing. MDM data can accompany this processing.

Finally, there is the new significant data store of NoSQL, supporting operational big data needs, as described in Chapter 10. There is data integration and data virtualization all over the place in the architecture, even in the operational space.

Moving to the post-operational side, we have Hadoop for analytical data with potential varying structure ("unstructured") that grows much more rapidly than the structured data in the data warehouse. We need to have the business capability to deal with Hadoop's data for this to be worthwhile. That will certainly be a gating factor to success.

Hadoop looks larger than the data warehouse, and it very well may be in terms of data size. In terms of importance, it very well may become a vital part of competitive advantage, but the data warehouse usually is quite important today and its advancement is assured.

There still may be cubes, although these structures implemented for performance, although their advantages have been trumped over time. There will certainly be a data warehouse, although consolidation may mean one or fewer than before.

The data warehouse ecosystem within information architecture may include relational, row-based, "normal" database management systems, data warehouse appliances, a separate columnar database, in-memory databases, or utilization of in-memory capabilities. As much as we are moving into heterogeneity—a familiar concept of this book—market offerings are consolidating necessary features like in-memory and columnar capabilities to the point of mitigating some of the diversity of structure. Nonetheless, it will be important to implement these capabilities, wherever they may be, for the right workloads.

And, oh yes, all of the above could be in a cloud or clouds. Ultimately, no two architectures will appear the same with all of these variables. The key to architecture— and, consequently, business success—is allocation of workloads to the right platforms and tying it all together meaningfully.

●●●————————————————————————————

Companies continually develop good architecture, but it usually happens in a series of "two steps forward, one step back" moves over time. Eventually, the criteria of architectural progress, defined in Chapter 1 as performance, fast performance, and scalability, are improved. The goal of this book is to accelerate your progress toward good architecture and eliminate the steps backward.

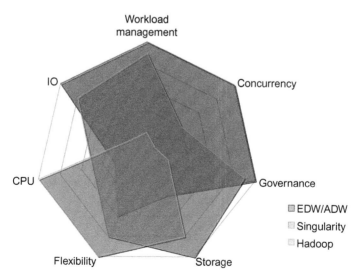

Figure 14.3 How eBay determines best fit of a workload to a large data platform.[3]

INFORMATION MANAGEMENT MATURITY

With all this movement afoot and all the endless possibilities, I give you some conceptual information about what brings companies to the architectural table and how you need to progress with your maturity. Without architecture, you might as well skip to the next chapter on business intelligence and just keep expanding the data access layer instead of the data platform layer. That is a loser's game. It reminds me of a passage in the book "Thinking Fast and Slow," which explains that we try hard just to do the expedient and not to think:

"System 1 provides the impressions that often turn into your beliefs, and is the source of the impulses that often become your choices and your actions. It offers a tacit interpretation of what happens to you and around you, linking the present with the recent past and with expectations about the near future. It contains the model of the world that instantly evaluates events as normal or surprising. It is the source of your rapid and often precise intuitive judgments. And it does most of this without your conscious awareness of its activities. System 1 is also, as we will see in the following chapters, the origin of many of the systematic errors in your intuitions."[1]

While, obviously, adding BI to our information architecture is the necessary last step, it is fast thinking and perhaps not the best (slow) thinking. BI is the "tip of the iceberg" of information management. The more leverageable and important work can be found in the "back end" of data warehouses, Hadoop, NoSQL stores, master data management, data stream processing, data virtualization, data warehouse appliances, with some strategically placed platforms and software in the cloud.

How Cisco will Improve its Information Management Maturity[2]

Year 0: Establish the vision, charter, goals, benefits, and roadmap.

Year 1: Establish oversight and execution teams; implement sustainable processes; identify success measures aligned with the business.

Year 2 +: Execute and evolve operations; drive continuous improvement; achieve best-in-class recognition for data management practices.

---

[1] Kahneman, Daniel (2011-10-25). Thinking, Fast and Slow (p. 58). Farrar, Straus and Giroux. Kindle Edition

[2] Source "Creating An Enterprise Data Strategy: Managing Data As A Corporate Asset": http://docs.media.bitpipe.com/io_10x/io_100166/item_417254/Creating%20an%20Enterprise%20Data%20Strategy_final.pdf

However, to be sure, all the information management back end (the focus of this book) is ultimately about supporting the BI. BI is what the users crave. Information management software sales teams understand this and commonly sell BI to the users, leaving the detail of getting the data act (the back end) together for an unsuspecting customer.

This is not necessarily an unseemly tactic since many sales teams do not understand architecture or the real work involved just to use a product. Even the "packaged" solutions typically require 50%–300% more work in data integration, data quality, and setup than is claimed, due to the ultimate uniqueness of companies. Information architecture is essential. You cannot simply acquire products in the shop and "stack" your way to success.

As much as a consultant might be able to truly see the future of an organization's needs, in the real world, it's hard to fix problems that aren't glaringly "in your face." Therefore, we have stages of progress.

There are steps in the maturity progression and they will be followed, whether we like it or not. In my maturity workshops and assessments, I move organizations to the next level and lay out a *plan* to Leadership. I do not take a Reactive organization and move them to Leadership in one week. However, with knowledge, you can move very quickly through the steps to Leadership, spending as little as a month in each Stage.

Organization size and age are not barometers for information management maturity.

Reactive Stage

In this stage, everything is "bottom up" and it is about reacting to the needs of the day. New applications get new databases. There is little reusability from past work and little focus on software maintenance or much of anything after the initial implementation. While there may not be a focus on maintenance and support, it exists. These necessities are treated as a surprise and crammed into the team's workload.

More importantly, there is no focus on architecture and, thus, no reuse is built into the architecture. This usually manifests itself in the "spaghetti" flow of data and the limited to no reusability of any data extract. Those who see no value proposition beyond the Reactive Stage will gloss over most of this book, except maybe to land on the next chapter on business intelligence topics.

Education is nonexistent and information management, as an extension of IT (which is usually an extension of something else), is completely off the radar as a necessary discipline. Phrases like "big data," "columnar databases," "master data management," "analytics," "data quality," "cloud computing," "self-service," "documentation," etc. are never heard in these organizations. Curiosity and creativity are low and the method for problem solving changes at a snail's pace.

There may be no data warehouse, although there may be some structures that are replicas of source structure that receive some data to "off-load" reporting. There is limited integration in any data store, but if there is any done, it is seen as a "one time only" need that will not need to be repeated ("Who needs integrated data?" may be heard).

Management lobs simple-sounding requests at IT,[3] but, in reality, without any informational foundation laid, these requests are hard. Often, IT will make a yeoman's effort to do the "one-time" report. This effort seldom gets back to the requesting management, furthering the incorrect impression that this is easy. And correct. I had one client who "covered up" the immense work these requests caused for years, until the executive raised some questions about the data and was irate to learn the process was not repeatable. He reflected on the decisions he had made with the data and determined that he had made wrong moves to the tune of several million dollars. Explain your work efforts and give management the chance to advocate change.

IT is a bottleneck in these organizations since the expedient "IT does it" mentality comes into play very quickly whenever anything remotely technical sounding is mentioned.

●●● ──

If you have a data warehouse, think about how the program started. Most likely, it was avoided until deep pain ensued.

──

This is a description of a worst-case scenario, obviously. These organizations clearly miss a lot of business value with their inattention to the important asset of information. They are also at a crossroads at which they are very susceptible to vendor product pitches ("cure-alls") for "sudden" perilous information needs. These might be accepted without reference to forming any architecture or processes to support the product,

---

[3] again, referring to those who do the function, not necessarily those in an organization with an "IT" title
[4] "Singularity" is an eBay homegrown platform; ignore for our purposes.

or light bulbs might go off which indicate that the organization is very much in the information business and needs to treat information as an asset.

In order to progress to the Repeatable Stage of Information Management maturity, an organization will:

- Understand and plan for the support and maintenance requirements of information management systems
- Reuse one or more data extracts by using them for different data stores
- At least one extract is scheduled and not considered "one-off"

Repeatable Stage

The feeds for those marts built for the one-offs that turned into repeatable needs might be systemized in the Repeatable Stage, a time when information begins to turn the corner and be seen as something that will need repeatable processes. Reports are recurring. Calculations are shared across multiple purposes.

Some variability in the business intelligence formats are being requested. IT is starting to get educated and speak up about the possibilities. "Analytics" and "data warehousing" may enter the vernacular and we may see a first-pass data warehouse: a copy of operational data onto a separate platform where concurrency with operations is not an issue and reporting can be pursued to the fullest. Data there may share a platform, but it is not integrated into the data model. For now, it's just data silos sharing a platform. Integration and data model revisions (perhaps substantial) will come into play for the Productive Stage.

●●●————————————————————————————————

Often companies will hit a wall trying to add the second internal "customer" to the data warehouse because they did not architect the data warehouse initially with scalable principles in mind. It does not take longer to do it right. It does, however, take knowledge.

————————————————————————————————

Reactive Stage tools may not be good enough anymore in the Repeatable Stage. Budgets begin to come in line with, although not quite completely to, the reality of the workload. A full life-cycle mentality that incorporates post-production and an iterative nature to information management may creep in.

There is no way that an organization can progress beyond the Repeatable Stage unless there is some leadership on the part of IT (bringing to bear the possibilities) and non-IT (colloquially referred to as the "business") brings their requirements to, and trusts, IT.

Ironically, occasionally it takes a screw up like a minor security breach to bring organizations to the next stage.

Productive Stage

Now we come to a critical juncture. Information is recognized as critical in all projects. There is a data warehouse. There may be a burgeoning master data management project. Basic analytics (see Chapter 3) are calculated, shared, and incorporated into business processes. Database options like in-memory and columnar are turned on and used— maybe not to the fullest, but the path has been started on.

One client, a large financial services firm, went through an exercise to determine how to utilize the latest features of their data warehouse DBMS, including in-memory and columnar. After implementing the changes, query times were reduced, on average, by 75%, some by 99%.

Non-data warehouse analytical data storage options emerge, but not always for the right reasons. Still-rogue business departments doing their own thing and decentralized but uninformed decision making may have brought some data warehouse appliances into the shop. It will require adjustment and some workload maneuvering to get to the Leadership Stage.

Data virtualization may or may not be utilized, since the habit of data integration is the first resort. There may be some optimization to be done here.

Master data management is not in place, at least not formally. MDM is not treated as a separate discipline. "Master data" comes together in the data warehouse, the one-way street, and is not shared back with the operational environment. The value of MDM would be clear, but it takes organizations some time to be ready for the MDM message.

No data stream processing or graph databases, yet. These may be foreign concepts, even at the Productive Stage of information management. Syndicated data is brought in for a single application or two into data marts, but not into any leverageable data store.

Big data may be discussed, both in the context of supporting operations as well as in the context of post-operational analytical data. Whatever big data is stored is selectively (by date or limited scale) stored in the data warehouse. However, there may be some "double secret" downloads of big data software like Hadoop happening for experimentation purposes.

One way or another, either from organizational directive or information management initiative, some data storage is happening in the cloud—perhaps some marts with unique characteristics or some of those still-rogue business departments doing their own thing have made it happen. This bottom-up cloud strategy will morph into a more heads-up approach that works best *for the organization* in the Leadership Stage.

The Productive Stage is, well, productive, for information management. It would certainly clear ROI hurdles if ever measured. Critical hurdles have been crossed and the organization is set up nicely for the Leadership Stage. IT is finally staying slightly ahead of the business community, but not by much.

It will require immense leadership to get the organization to the exponentially valuable Leadership Stage. This book is geared toward those who want to bring their organizations this kind of value.

Leadership Stage

In the Leadership Stage, the lens of information is very clear. All information within the organization is captured because all information can be used. Outside, syndicated information is brought in to leverageable data stores like an MDM hub.

The MDM hub is now in place for key subject areas, taking the formerly immense burden of coming up with this data for each application off of each application and replacing it with an "API"[5] approach. Best of all, the data is trusted.

Big data curiosity is replaced by big data projects. Big data solutions are necessary to capture all of the organization's data and then serve the data operationally and serve it up to analytics. Analytics is embraced in the Leadership Stage and embedded into all applications and business processes.

●●●
———————————————————————————————————————

One large telecommunications company was only able to find value in storing one month's worth of detailed call detail records in their data warehouse DBMS. By adopting Hadoop, they decided to store seven years' worth, and found value in doing so.

———————————————————————————————————————

Like MDM, Data Stream Processing is siphoning cycles and emphasis away from the data warehouse and toward a more real-time function. Speaking of the data warehouse, it is a mini-ecosystem now with elements of in-memory, columnar, and data temperature consideration spanning multiple databases.

[5] Application Programming Interface

In the Leadership Stage, no two companies' architectures are going to be the same. Though most of the data stores in this book are necessary in every Leadership Stage company, some will be embraced to different degrees than others. There will be a diversity of data stores in every Leadership Stage company as a result of the agile pursuit of information, and business, leadership.

Though it's never a primary focus, even in Leadership Stage companies, to "clean up" legacy messes, data warehouse consolidation will be done to reduce unnecessary and redundant stores and cube consolidation will be done to deemphasize these structures in favor of more targeted data stores.

A corporate cloud strategy, or at least an Information Management one, is in place; it is a hybrid strategy (Chapter 13) and the strategy is being realized. At decision points for information management software and hardware, the decisions consider the cloud strategy.

In addition, illustrating the importance of information to the bottom line, the CIO has a seat in the boardroom.

Finally, these companies will pursue their projects using agile strategies and organization change management and with collaboration and self-service approaches to business intelligence, which also incorporates mobile platforms. Read on to the last three chapters for more information on these leadership enablers.

●●●──

Do the stage descriptions above sound too specific? Too descriptive? I've been in information management my whole career and have performed close to 100 Assessments in which I review an organization's progress and get them to the next level, with a plan to become leaders in information and leaders in business. It is uncanny how closely maturity follows the paths I outline here. I anticipate this to be the case for many years to come.

LEADERSHIP

Leadership is the ability to impress, guide, and challenge people toward common goals. What I said about information management leadership in 2008 is true today:

"More demonstrated leadership would help secure funding, leverage vendors, and establish partnerships with the business that would uncover true business requirements. It would increase the confidence of information management personnel in leadership positions to make organizational suggestions for improvement, to bring in new technologies and processes and, importantly, to gain a greater depth of vision with which to provide ROI to the business. Leadership gives more leash to information management undertakings, allowing for some limited deferral for business gains. The switchover from non-credible, lights-on tactical information management to a credible source of potential business ROI happens with the maturity and success of the business, but it does not happen without demonstrated leadership."[6]

I get concerned when my clients want to tightly hold the reins and fade into the wallpaper. That is a losing strategy. At the end of the day, information management leadership is all about personal leadership. Only through personal leadership can the progress be made to support a company to compete with information.

ACTION PLAN

- Diagram your current information architecture
- Diagram a 3-year, currently desired future state information architecture
- Know which stage of maturity you are in
- Study what it takes to get to the next stage
- Develop specific action plans to achieve that stage; it will be uncannily consistent with improving the business
- Take a keen focus on leadership; your personal education should not be strictly technical

[6]http://www.information-management.com/issues/2007_48/10001363-1.html

Modern Business Intelligence— Collaboration, Mobile, and Self-Service: Organizing the Discussion and Tethering the User to Information

The data stores we are talking about in this book find their true value in an enterprise when the data is put to use. For most of the data access, that means a human[1] fetches the data for a unique use or utilizes a predefined data access such as a report. The old saw about business intelligence is that it gets "the right information to the right people at the right time." It's really time to add "in the right medium" to that mix. While this business intelligence ability is an entire discipline unto itself beyond information management, I felt it important to provide some guidance here, since it is the discipline that will utilize the information we manage.

Business intelligence is the sizzle to information management's steak. It is the final step in data's life cycle, and it must be done well. However, keep in mind that getting the data act together is 80% of the business intelligence battle. You simply cannot do business intelligence well without a robust information management infrastructure.[2]

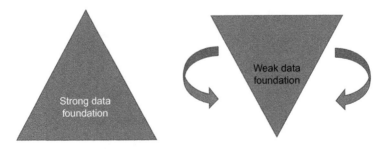

Figure 15.1 Business Intelligence without a strong data foundation is easily toppled.

[1] Referred to as a "user." Only information technology and the drug professions—legal and illegal—refer to their customers as users, but that is what they are normally called. Again, I'm trying not to invent new terminology in the book, but to help you successfully stay educated.
[2] Despite the claims of BI-only vendors

There are information stores that are exceptions to the rule of primarily serving user data access. Stream processing (Chapter 8) is a fully automated way of storing the data. Master data management does have a data access component, but primarily serves its data to other systems. Some of the NoSQL stores support operations directly as well.

There are numerous ways to fetch the data. The most basic and limited, yet still the most used, is reporting.

The accepted paradigm of effective business intelligence must change. Once it was exclusively reports built by IT from overnight-batch-loaded data warehouses, which replicated a single or small set of source systems. Those reports were deployed to the personal computers of "users" in what seems like, in hindsight, a very heavy-handed and resource-intensive process.

Just getting a report to a user's personal computer on a regular basis is nowhere near the pinnacle of business intelligence achievement. Shops with this mentality are leaving tremendous value on the table.

Now, the considered norm for business intelligence involves "zero footprint" web-based delivery of reports. This improvement allows information to reach many more users. However, increasingly it has been noted that while the detailed, transactional data is absolutely necessary to be accessible on a drill-through basis, it is the rapid availability of summary level information that activates the process.

A majority of users have become more accustomed to a targeted presentation layer. Dashboards represent an advanced form of information delivery, second only to operational business intelligence as a mature approach to disseminating information. Building dashboards that already have a certain amount of knowledge worker intelligence built-in moves the organization towards real-time competitiveness.

I'm not going to delve into great reporting practices here because enterprises have largely evolved to the best practices for their shop. Detethering enterprises from basic reporting (query to database to screen) and into these more evolved forms of data access is going to be necessary for information management success. Today, this means considering the mobile user and incorporating collaborative features into the data access function and enabling a climate of "self-serve" unabated access for the user to the data.

THE MOBILE REVOLUTION

The fix is in. Most, corporate workers and IT professionals understand that mobile-based applications will surpass traditional computing platforms in terms of users, application deployments, and enterprise importance. This will happen in the enterprise in the near future.

Think of mobility as the next huge wave for technology, following on the internet wave of the 2000s, which was preceded by personal computing, mini computing, and mainframe computing waves dating back to the 1960s. The mobile movement will extend to billions of people worldwide. It will advance in good times and as it will during regressive environments, during which time mobility will begin to replace landlines. It will have far more impact than the tethered, desktop internet.

With mobility, information is available without limits. Every location is like an office in some sense. The graying of the line between work and non-work continues in earnest. To some, this can cause grief, but it is a definite trend and represents a mindset for success in the workplace in the next decade—taking care of business when you can.

Mobile business intelligence is both portable, like paper-based reports, and interactive (and green) like internet-based activity.

Mobile devices continue to advance tremendously in terms of sheer computing power, capacity, speed, capabilities, and innovative techniques unique to the platform. With widespread public, enterprise, and private availability, Wi-Fi continues to blanket the planet, creating inexpensive ways to stay connected. The latest "generation" of networks goes mainstream very quickly.

"Apps" have become the new method of delivering. With highly focused functionality, apps deliver self-selected interesting functions that, in the aggregate, have vast adoption. As a means of accomplishing tasks quickly, apps have no peer. What works in the real world works in enterprises, and mobile devices are the embodiment of what enterprise information users want. The impact of mobility on business intelligence expectations means more than quick accomplishment of tasks. It also means solutions must deliver for:

- Low Latency—users will not tolerate slow response times
- An increased User Population—more people wanting to do more things with BI

Like water, information and analytics must flow through the path of least resistance, utilizing the deployment option that turns the information into valuable business action most quickly.

We have different expectations of and cognitive and emotional attachments to different devices. For example, we expect to do full, unabated authoring on the personal computer, little authoring on the cell phone, and somewhere in between for the tablet and other hybrids.

Drill-through is the expected paradigm of data access on mobile. Mobile does make an excellent notification platform as long as it allows drill-through to detail.

Its "always on" nature alleviates the problem of real-time information delivered to an abandoned desktop, or to the web—with or without notice—that inherently involves multiple steps for the user to derive value and does not capitalize on available, real-time information. The answer is mobile business intelligence, or utilizing the mobile device as the data access layer.

MOBILE BUSINESS INTELLIGENCE

Today's enterprise has dispersed workers, virtual offices, and global presences.

When it comes to implementing mobile business intelligence, it will be more than a shrunken web- or desktop-based screen. Screen renderings will need to be delivered that make the best use of the space in a drill-down mentality. It should all provide functionality for all of the multitouch gestures that Apple and their ilk have gotten us used to through trial and error. These gestures include:

- Tap
- Swype
- Flick
- Double Tap
- Rotate
- Pinch
- Touch & Drag
- Two Finger Swype
- Touch & Hold

This makes a compelling argument for buying a mobile-enabled business intelligence platform as it will have the gestures built in. You will simply need to design—or review the recommendations for—each gesture.[3]

Other benefits and differences for mobile business intelligence is integration with the mapping programs on the mobile device for location awareness, integration with other apps on the device, and ability to utilize the information capture for QR codes, accelerometer data, bar code readers, and speech recognition.

---

[3] Although it must be noted that not all mobile BI solutions are created equal; their capabilities and levels of interactivity may differ, as may their performance

Today's enterprise has dispersed workers, virtual offices, and global presences. Today's enterprise needs agility in information access and needs to be able to make decisions as soon as possible, and it needs empowered and collaborative workers. Mobile business intelligence is becoming an important part of the BI environment everywhere.

There are definitely challenges in rolling out mobile device support in an enterprise, let alone for mobile business intelligence. Those challenges include standards, the battery life, and signal loss. But, to be sure, mobile phones and tablet computers are business devices. They provide real-time business mobility. They allow users to abandon their desktops, which is what they need to do anyway, and there is little to no information loss in going to mobile.

Each organization must address its support infrastructure and mobile security needs in terms of which devices they will support and how to encourage the right security policies around encryption and cash credentials. This may necessitate the mandating of policies for remote wiping and password authorization of devices.

You can mobilize your existing reports. You can mobilize your dashboards. BI on mobile devices may be easier to integrate into your work processes than you think. Many business intelligence applications are being built exclusively for a mobile user today.

SELF-SERVICE BUSINESS INTELLIGENCE

By definition, it's almost not analysis if an abstracted third party like IT personnel are heavily involved in data access.

On the opposite end of the spectrum, the business intelligence setup can almost anticipate the analyst session with the data. Rudimentary actions that would be taken based on a shallow view of data have already been thought of and taken in these environments. Those actions have been built into the environment, along with the standard business rules needed by the analyst. What's left is highly substantial interactive analysis. If supported by modeled and clean data and a user-friendly interface, the analysis can go quite deep.

While leaving the appropriate analysis to the analyst, but removing the data collection and navigation hurdles, these sessions are much more productive.

Not only must the analysis go deep in order to keep a company competitive, each company must become more efficient in time spent by both IT and the (non-IT) business areas. The model of giving users the choice of (1) shallow analysis or (2) heavy IT/BI team involvement in analysis is not going to last much longer. Self-service BI techniques are necessary.

Self-service business intelligence can be viewed positively or negatively. To some, it's a positive term connoting the removal of barriers to a goal. However, to some, "self-service" is a negative term, euphemistically meaning "no service" or "you're on your own." Self-service BI is about removing barriers and reliance on parties and processes that would stand between a user and his or her data.

If you put up a data store that is simply a copy of other data, only lightly remodeled from source, it usually carries many of the same data quality flaws of the source. It solves a big problem—making the data available—but after this copy of data, the fun begins with each new query being a new adventure into data sources, tools, models, etc. What has inevitably happened in some environments is that users take what they need, like it's raw data, and do the further processing required for the business department or function.

This post-storage processing is frequently very valuable to the rest of the organization—if the organization could only get access to it. However, data that is generated and calculated post-data warehouse has little hope of reaching any kind of shared state. This data store is not ready for self-service BI.

To achieve these goals, you need a solid foundation and solid processes. Take account of your BI environment. While IT and consultancy practices have coined "self-service business intelligence" to put some discipline to the idea of user empowerment, some of it is mere re-labeling of "no service" BI and does not attain and maintain a healthy relationship with the user community or healthy exploitation of the data produced in the systems. We all know that IT budgets are under pressure, but this is not the time to cut vital services of support that maintain multimillion dollar investments. We will explore this deeper in the chapter on Organizational Change Management.

Self-service business intelligence is good for the bottom line, too.

In business intelligence, data integration is the most time-consuming part of the build process. This is undeniably true. However, if one were to look at the long-term, most long-term costs clearly fall into the data access layer. This is where the reports, dashboards, alerts, etc. are built.

Self-service BI is a mentality, not a set of tools, but there are tools that support this notion of self-service better than others. These tools attack a very important component of the long-term cost of BI—the cost of IT having to continue to do everything post-production.

There are a few areas that signify BI tools that work best with a user self-service mindset:

1. They perform fast—this allows a user, in the few minutes of time he or she has, to do an analysis to get to a deeper level of root cause analysis
2. They are seen as more intuitive—this empowers the end user so they can do more, versus getting IT involved, which stalls a thought stream and introduces delay that can obliterate the relevancy
3. They deploy fast—you can get to basic analysis very quickly and work your way into deeper analysis as needed over time
4. They offer collaboration, explained below

Self-Service BI and Outsourced BI

To truly set up business intelligence to work in a self-service capacity, you would overweigh the idea of working closely with users in the build process, which is a lever that gets deemphasized in outsourced BI. You would see business intelligence as less a technical exercise and more as an empowerment exercise. You would keep the build closer to home, where the support would be. And you would not gear up an offshore group to handle a laborious process of maintaining the data layer over the years in the way users desire. You would invest in users—culture, education, information use—instead of outsourced groups. And this is just what many are doing now.

COLLABORATIVE BUSINESS INTELLIGENCE

"Self-service business intelligence" is a good catchphrase for where BI needs to go. Tangibly, in addition to modeled, clean data and a "user friendly" interface, self-service BI (or at least most of the tools claiming the category) offer collaboration.

If you have recently done BI business requirements, measured BI ROI, or tracked BI usage through to the business action, you can see the value of collaboration. Other than collaboration, self-service BI tools exploit memory adeptly so they offer better performance and the UI is seen as more intuitive.

I tend to think it's the performance and collaboration that is most useful to users. Tool vendors may need to look beyond the user interface for their next release big splashes. Simpler UIs are in demand. Consider the Facebook interface. It's simple, but used by 750 million users. Content, performance, and collaboration are king.

Elements of collaboration include an embedded discussion forum or a workflow component, making it easy and delay-free for the user community to cooperate and partner together to reach business conclusions. It includes star ratings, simple comments, interactivity, interfaces to internal social networks, unstructured data, security, and bookmarks. Sound familiar? Sounds like a modern web session to me.

Collaborative BI is the combination of Collaborative Interaction, Information Enhancement, and Collaborative Decision Making. It is collecting and memorializing the communication over data that would naturally occur otherwise. It facilitates that communication and accelerates it. Communication that would normally require phone calls and emails,[4] can now happen within the confines of business intelligence. Communication enhances the value of the information assets we bring to the enterprise.

Among the elements of good collaborative BI are:
- Commenting
- Annotation
- Discussion
- Report Approval Workflow
- Prompts to action

Naturally, not all solutions that claim to be collaborative have all of these features.

Whether the scope of the collaboration is a data element or one of its uses, as in a report, is significant and requires design. For example, if a report is sales by region by month for this year, when does a comment about a low-performing region show up—for the report and/or the period and/or the region? Collaboration must be designed in this way.

Another good practice is to encourage face-to-face or virtual meetings among users where there is a high concentration of collaboration activity. This indicates an ongoing, and unresolved, conversation, and a meeting could be best for attaining closure.

---

[4]Email is an awkward medium for these communications; automated messages are worse. Newer social technologies, however, have the potential to do much better.

Collaborative BI mirrors social media. Another artifact of good collaborative BI is voting buttons whereby decisions over data can be voted upon. Also, users can "follow" reports or their collaboration in much the same way people follow blogs and/or the blog comments. Users can follow "subjects," machines, customers, regions, etc.

Users are also represented in a familiar way—with their picture!

Collaborative business intelligence, combined with a great data foundation, makes the very most of the limited analysis window of the user. Collaborative features should be considered essential in any business intelligence rollout accessing our information management stores.

Thinking Still Required

Despite my admonitions to automate business intelligence where possible and to bring the data access to a fuller level of readiness to serve the user through exception-based dashboards and intelligent use of smaller screen sizes, nothing replaces the value that the end user brings to the analysis of the data.

The question is not whether or not business intelligence systems will be able to truly think. Of course, they will not. Nor is the question whether or not BI systems will be able to create the illusory effect of thinking. Skillful business intelligence architects already create systems that pack enough "wow" effect to achieve a temporary transcendence for them. They will also clearly get better at it. Business intelligence displays apparently intelligent behavior when it automatically alters in-process promotions to be rerouted to prospect profiles that are responding to the initial mailing. When business intelligence reroutes procedures to best-of-breed providers, it is displaying intelligence. Additionally, when it changes pricing automatically in response to demand, it is displaying intelligence and providing extreme value to the enterprise.

ACTION PLAN

- Assess the benefit of mobility to current business intelligence
- Assess the mobile strategy of your business intelligence vendors
- Consider the mobile option for all new business intelligence requirements
- Determine if collaboration is happening over business intelligence and the benefits that collaboration within the tools could bring

- Assess the collaboration capabilities of your business intelligence tools
- Give users more roles and responsibilities in business intelligence, up to the level they can handle, and then some

CHAPTER SIXTEEN

Agile Practices for Information Management

I have been extensively covering information architecture possibilities and the end result that is desired, with only passing mention of the process of how to get there. Now that you are formulating the information architecture for your organization, getting there will be the focus of this chapter.

Naturally, we have been careful to avoid unnecessary latencies in the architecture, making sure that data moves as quickly as it can to where it can be effective. Delivering high performance has practically been the primary driver of the book and, as previously mentioned, is a primary focus in architecture development. Again, we need to do all we can to promote the very important asset of information, removing obstacles even at the cost of some added technology.

The Time-Value Curve (Figure 16.1) is about architectural latencies, but what about delivery latencies? There is another obstacle that keeps many a user away from his data and that has to do with the time it takes to deliver projects on-target to user need. Hopefully by now, as an information manager, you are convinced that you have a lot of work ahead of you. There is no time for the unnecessary, the inefficient, or rework.

For quite some time I have been breaking up otherwise long projects into smaller projects for delivery. I want my teams to stay as close as possible to delivering to production, which is what it's all about. I also understand that, despite good requirements gathering, the best feedback comes in the form of reviewing actual work that you are calling somewhat complete.

Those predilections turned out to be a perfect match for the era of agile methodologies. I'm on board! I have seen otherwise good teams become great teams when some components of agile are assimilated. The one I have adopted is SCRUM.[1] Though these methodologies started with software development and not in-house enterprise development, they have serious applicability.

[1] With apologies to Extreme Programming and Agile Unified Process

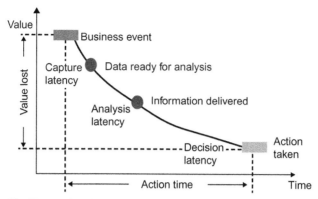

Figure 16.1 The Time-Value Curve, Richard Hackathorn, Boulder Technology, Inc.

I don't, however, think you need to become SCRUM-certified, attend weeks of training, adopt the terminology in a strict sense, or have every team member count backwards beginning with their birth year or else be demoted a belt color to be effective. Some of the adoption is counterproductive. I continually see shops going overboard with agile as if it's all-or-nothing. It is my attempt in this chapter to give you the "best of" SCRUM for your information management projects. After all, it's all about delivering to production.

TRADITIONAL WATERFALL METHODOLOGY

Traditional waterfall methodologies incur too much cost, rework, and risk to be effective in the dynamic field of information management. ROI tends to be delayed too long. Agile methodologies balance out the risk (and reward) over time. Some of the ways SCRUM does this is through taking "how do we handle this?" questions off the table. To a very high degree, everyone knowing the rules of the game makes for a much better game. But, you say, all methodologies do this. True, good ones do, but let me expose the elements of SCRUM that make it balanced.

We must maintain a balance between rigor and creativity (see Figure 16.2 "Unbalanced Methodologies"). That's where leadership and judgment come into play and no methodology will ever replace that! Any methodology that claims you just put the people into place and it works without major decision making along the way, is folly. As I discuss agile approaches, and SCRUM

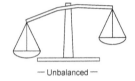

· Project management   · Creativity
· Change management   · Open
· Time management   · Quick response
· Documentation   · Adhoc
· Testing   — Unbalanced — · Flexible
· Budgeting   · Reactive
· Planning   · New advanced
· Standards   technology
· ROI Metrics

Figure 16.2 Unbalanced Methodologies.

in particular, please note I am not discounting the need for leadership and judgment in the process.

AGILE APPROACHES

The now somewhat-famous Agile Manifesto has become the foundation of several methodologies, including SCRUM. It simply reads:

- Individuals and interactions over processes and tools
- Working software over comprehensive documentation
- Customer collaboration over contract negotiation
- Responding to change over following a plan

The principles behind the Agile Manifesto include: early and continuous delivery of valuable software, delivery of working software frequently, business people and developers working together,[2] projects built around motivated individuals, simplicity is essential, self-organizing teams, and regular reflection and tuning.

Your judgment and leadership will have to come into play here to determine to what degree you take it. Many organizations are forcing the issue by adopting SCRUM company-wide, which makes it easy as to which profile you take on:

- Company-wide adoption of SCRUM with obvious effects on the business intelligence program
- Information technology-wide adoption of SCRUM
- Information management-wide adoption of some level of agile/SCRUM principles

I suggest the last bullet is the minimum requirement, so I will delve into some applicable aspects of SCRUM for information management.

---

[2] The last chapter, on Organizational Change Management, will help with this

SCRUM

SCRUM has forged an immense amount of new terminology. Perhaps the best way to share the methodology is to review it term by term. Please note, in so doing, I am suggesting the right level of SCRUM to adopt. It's a means to an end. It's not the gold-rimmed, overdone version, nor is it just picking off some concepts and calling it a methodology.

SCRUM purists will be beside themselves reading this and arguing that I forgot the 23rd principle and that people really need 3 weeks of training and passing tests and whatnot to be agile. If you want to go down that route, it's available out there. I certainly don't need to repeat that material here.

As with the technology chapters, implementation will require more in-depth training for the immediate technology team. With SCRUM, a shop may want to consider some web-based or in-person training for a few who will fill key roles, with the understanding that they will do on-the-job just-in-time training for the rest of the participants on their projects. All SCRUM training should be taken with the filter on that I present here.

Likewise, those new to SCRUM may find the terminology awkward and want to lessen the rigor I suggest here. While I can agree it's ultimately about results, I can only suggest a level based on my vast experience running, consulting on, and auditing information management projects. I may bend some after learning of a unique situation, but far too often people will jump to the "but we're unique" argument when it is not warranted.

This is a balanced, information management-focused interpretation of SCRUM. It's a version that tends to get used by successful shops after they start at one of the unbalanced ends.

By the way, while you may exercise this terminology within the team, do not expect the rest of the organization to necessarily engage in it or even care about the methodology. They will care about results.

"It's better to be roughly right than precisely wrong." John Maynard Keynes

Product

A product is a long-term deliverable and comprises releases (which are comprised of sprints). A product is what goes into budget cycles and what gets upper management excited, promoted, and fired. A product can take a year or more to complete. A product is SCRUM's link to waterfall methodologies. Whereas a project comes into being in much the same way in both camps, from that point forward, SCRUM treats a project quite differently.

Release

A release is best thought of as sitting between the product and the sprint. It may be a key milestone in a project. It is something that upper management is interested in as a "project milestone." It's a multimonth delivery that will show progress toward the product.

Sprint

OK, here we go. A sprint is 2–4 weeks (2 weeks is best) of activity by the SCRUM team. There are several requirements (user stories) that the team is trying to be accomplish in the sprint. The sprint is characterized by daily semi-structured meetings and detailed tracking of the percentage complete of each story (requirement, explained below). A sprint is also the level that should be communicated to the organization-at-large in terms of what the team is going to accomplish ("failure is not an option!" mentality) in the sprint. If the sprint does not include shippable (to users/systems) components, they need to be "potentially shippable." You would need to decide what this means in the context of your project, but it should be a high bar, as in going to production and being used.

User Stories

User stories are requirements in the most granular form. Stories are negotiated by the team and the Product Owner in the Sprint Planning meeting at the transition point between sprints. Stories may be themed and longer stories are called epics. All stories will be assigned story points which represent the relative effort required to complete the story. This minimizes long cycles of acute time planning, opting instead for educated speculation.

What Makes a Good User Story
- Independent
- Negotiable
- Valuable
- Able to be Estimated
- Sized Appropriately
- Testable

Impediments

In the daily SCRUM meetings, each person is asked for progress on stories as well as impediments, which are tasks to be done by others (internal or external) or waiting periods to wait out something that is impeding one's progress against his or her assigned stories.

Product Roadmap

This is the SCRUM version of the iteration plan. It's a lightly shared document owned by the Product Owner that is a working, directional estimate of what foreseeable future sprints will be comprised of.

Team Capacity

Team Capacity is how much work product the SCRUM team can deliver in a sprint. Obviously, it's not an assembly line, so there is a lot of judgment involved. Team Capacity is measured by something called story points, described below.

Sprint Backlog

Those stories accepted into a sprint become the sprint backlog. It's a very manageable list that the SCRUM Team can keep top of mind throughout the sprint. Once stories are accepted into a sprint, they cannot be changed. This is partly punitive and instructive for the process that takes on stories, but primarily it is a relief for the SCRUM team, knowing that their work is stable. For two weeks.

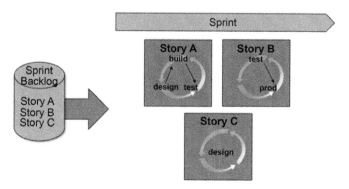

Figure 16.3 Many stories per sprint, in different stages, at least one to production.

Product Backlog

This is a place where anybody in the company can add a story. This accumulates over time and only abates as stories are pulled into sprints and delivered.

Daily SCRUM Meetings

Literally daily meetings at a set time in a set room (and/or with set conference/internet call coordinates) for all of the SCRUM team. All team members take turns taking the floor answering the following questions: What did you do yesterday? What are you working on today? Any impediments?

Sprint Burn Down

Stories on the sprint backlog are "burned down" by increasing the percentage completion daily as they are worked on. Everyone can, therefore, have a good sense of progress because the entire sprint will therefore have a math-based "overall percentage completion." A graph can easily show[3] where progress is and where it needs to be on a sprint.

Sprint Planning Meeting

The pre- (or post- since they occur simultaneously) meeting of the SCRUM team and the sprint master to review the product backlog and build the sprint backlog. It's a participatory process whereby all may help estimate the size of the story. Obviously, only so many stories (up to a predetermined limit) can be accepted into a sprint. Story points are used as surrogates for capacity and work effort. Philosophically, the total story points are what the collective team needs to deliver. The team will win or lose together based on this. If, during the sprint, team members need to pitch in for one another—usually because of slight under- and overestimation in the story points, that is expected. So, there are significant team aspects to the estimation.

Story Points

"Story points" is also a SCRUM concept that may be unfamiliar to someone coming from waterfall approaches. What the heck is 3 story points, anyway? What's important here is not "how many" points, but consistency of point allocation across the stories and over time. All team members may opt in on estimating EACH story in the sprint—even ones they will not personally touch. It's "1-2-3-show" and fingers or cards are revealed. Discrepancies are discussed until ONE value per story is reached.

---

[3] Many SCRUM programs are managed with Project Tracking Software that facilitates the tracking

SCRUM Story Point Estimation

Many use the Fibonacci sequence of numbers (1, 2, 3, 5, 8, 13, 21, etc.). This works because it's easier to estimate the short stories so there's more granularity possible there (1, 2, 3, 5 points). As the stories get harder and longer, they are naturally more difficult to estimate, so they are estimated at only certain intervals. There should be an upper limit on story points assigned (i.e., 21, 34). Over that, stories should be broken up. The SCRUM guideline for this in terms of hours is 16 hours estimated maximum per story.

Others use an estimate of total team hours on the story, which I am not going to say is as bad to do as some will. After all, it does come down to time. Others use shirt sizes (S, M, L, XL, XXL), etc. or dog breeds (from Chihuahua to Terrier to Great Dane). For fun, I've used balls (marble, ping pong, tennis, baseball, softball, volleyball, soccer ball, basketball, beach ball). Obviously, the aggregate levels for the sprint need to be understood as well. That's why you end up with straight-faced discussions that contain "So, in this sprint, we are committing to three beach balls of stories." This is only limited by imagination. I'd be interested in how you do it, so let us know in the comments.

While there is clearly a science to the process I spoke of, judgment remains essential for SCRUM success. If you go into sprint planning looking for 29 story points and the points land you at 27 and the smallest story point count you have left is 3, should you add it or not? Judgment. Prerequisites must also be considered. Stories have prerequisites and, while the goal is to deliver a complete "product" of sorts in the sprint, the reality is that there are often multiple threads (i.e., source systems, sets of business rules, sets of reports, etc.) that are being worked on at any point in time.

Figure 16.4 Sprint Reciprocal Commitments.

Sprint Retrospective

A meeting of the SCRUM Team immediately following each sprint which, like the other meetings, solicits input from each team member. In this case, there are three questions that each team member responds to:
- What worked?
- What did not work?
- How to improve?

Product Owner

This is the involved person representing the business interests. With the right, but not obligation, to attend the daily meetings, the Product Owner keeps the business interest top of mind. It is possible for one person to be product owner of multiple sprints and products.

SCRUM Master

The SCRUM Master has a high understanding of the SCRUM process and makes sure that it is followed by the team. The SCRUM Master does not have to have anything except a cursory understanding of the information management domain being worked on in the sprint, although the more, the better. The SCRUM Master runs the daily meetings and typically will run the project and report progress to upper management quantitatively and dispassionately.

SCRUM Team

A team of 5–8 who are brought together to work on a sprint, and usually a series (or years) of sprints toward product completion. Being multitalented is a great quality of a SCRUM team member since priorities change from sprint to sprint and the team member continuity is important. For example, many information management professionals can handle data integration and data delivery, so their focus may change from sprint to sprint according to the needs of that sprint.

SCRUM AND METHODOLOGY THEMES
Multitasking

In SCRUM, there is an eschewing of multitasking in favor of focus. Studies of multitasking show a serious drop-off in doing value-added work once the number of tasks exceeds 2. In SCRUM, individuals are focused for the duration of the sprint on "1" task (1 is in quotes because we know how nuanced information management tasks can be).

Scoping Small Enough

Stories must be broken down to fit into sprints. Although many people can contribute to a story, most are fit for one person to deliver, or at least be on point for. Breaking down stories into this fine a grain will be done by the team prior to developing the sprint backlog. The collective team will need a strong sense of the tasks to be done to build information management.

Other Challenges

Many of the things I have encountered in my journey to agile include lack of attendance at the stand-ups at first, programmers estimating with huge buffering (for the worst case scenarios), and a need to hone the stories and tasks in a meaningful way. I can look at one graph and tell how a project is doing now, but this is only after I learned the balance between task size and too many tasks. In short, when the tasks are too large and developers log hours against the tasks day after day, it is difficult to tell if, indeed, the task is nearing completion.

"Letting go as a leader" comes with the "self-managing teams" concept. Often, a Scrum Master that does not have domain knowledge can still be very effective.

The definition of "done" can be challenging to get consensus on. Sprints, and stories and tasks, in the project need clear definitions of exit criteria.

Please note that this is all only referring to project work in terms of using SCRUM. Production work—the arguably more important half of the team's workload—is still more queue-based work.

Keep a focus on quality, too. Two weeks often is simply too short a time to deliver complete information management, let alone complete many data integration cycles. You could enlarge the duration of the sprint, but I've found that 2 weeks is the best cadence to work scope around. However, too high a focus on delivering a sprint could cause good methodology compromise. If you compromise data quality, metadata, architecture, and other forms of essential value, you may win the sprint battle, but lose the information management war.

To achieve agility for the users, you need not only an agile process, but also tools that are aligned with this approach. It would be a shame to deliver quickly, while users still experience poor performance. Deliver information agility with agile.

Some characteristics of agile tools are:

- Intuitive and easy to use
- Fast
- Interactive
- Works with any data
- Self-service

ACTION PLAN

- Immediately update any waterfall methodology (or no methodology) for information management to be agile—SCRUM preferably—according to the direction in this chapter
- Identify a SCRUM Master who will perform the function across information management projects
- Identify Product Owners for all discrete information management projects
- Identify an upcoming information management project to execute with SCRUM, understanding that there is a learning curve well worth getting past

CHAPTER SEVENTEEN

Organizational Change Management: The Soft Stuff is the Hard Stuff

I would be remiss in providing a complete formula for information success if I left off the most important factor of all—people. That's right, moving workloads to the most effective platforms, utilizing the cloud, setting up the business intelligence, and doing it all in agile fashion, is all for naught without taking care of the people issues.

Information management brings organizational change. There is change in the way decisions are made, in the way data is accessed, in processes around data, and ultimately in company direction and performance. Most organizations, even in the Global 2000,[1] will be completely transformed by information management in the next decade. Whether your company will go there quickly and willingly is the only question.

This chapter presents managing organizational change as a practice—Organizational Change Management (OCM). OCM takes care of the important people issues of information management and empowers information managers to gain acceptance of their work products by introducing a set of supporting work products to manage the change.

With permission, parts of this chapter have been pulled from "Soft Issues, Hard Work" by William McKnight, *Teradata Magazine*.

●●●
————————————————————————————

"Without people, profit numbers mean squat…it's the by-product of taking care of people." – *Ken Blanchard, at Leadership Conference*

————————————————————————————

The disparity between expecting change and feeling able to manage it—the "Change Gap"—is growing at an unprecedented pace. This has put a lot of shops into traction as they leap into the projects they need to do to stay competitive, yet remain concerned about the ultimate acceptance of those projects by the organization. To be successful, these projects will need to

[1] Annual ranking of the top 2000 public companies in the world by Forbes magazine

change the organization. Projects that master change are highly correlated to success. However, to be successful in times of change, wishful thinking will not fill the change gap.

There is nowhere like information management (IM) projects to bring out the need for changing attitudes and mindsets. Changing information by consolidating it into a data warehouse or a master data management hub, applying rules to "fix" the data quality, or implementing workflow/ sharing mechanisms requires unprecedented organizational change. The complexities of engaging in behavioral and organizational change in these projects are too often underestimated. This happens at peril. It truly is the "soft stuff" that's hard.

I will now review a set of work products that should be included in the course of information management projects to ensure that the technical work product results are accepted and ultimately achieve their goals.

ORGANIZATIONAL CHANGE MANAGEMENT WORK PRODUCTS

Stakeholder Management Determines Who Will be Affected by the Change

Stakeholders to IM projects come from various parts of the organization and beyond. The perceptions of these "interested parties" of the project will ultimately determine your ability to declare your project a success. Of course, we all put the direct users into this category. Intellectually. However, practically, do we treat this diverse crowd as if they hold the power that they do? Stakeholder Analysis helps ensure that we do.

The obvious stakeholders are in positions of leadership directly over and directly affected by the information management project. With these leaders especially, it is important to model the behavior you want them to adopt. If the impending change is not given priority by you, why would they make it a priority? As such, there may be some special measures necessary in the care of these executives, as opposed to other stakeholders. Executive care must be planned, not haphazard.

Stakeholders also come from indirect users of the information, such as external customers, supply chain partners, suppliers, vendors, partners, your users' management, and the executive management of the company. Though they may not directly "use" or contribute to the new information, these people are affected by the implementation of IM as well. In most cases, the IM implementation is really about these people and the "users" are really using IM to support these stakeholders. Any stakeholder analysis should go to this level.

Stakeholder Management will address a number of key questions:

Who

- Who are the Stakeholders? (Name, Role, Contact information, Location, Impact, Influence)

What

- What do they know about the project? (Keep in mind, business leaders are prone to rash judgment and it may take work to move a mindset)
- What actions may they take to support the project?
- What actions may they take to derail the project?
- What about this project affects their success in their role?
- What actions do we need to take to influence them in the way we would like?

Where

- Where are they now? Are they supportive/negative/neutral now? By how much?
- Where are the stakeholder locations?

When

- When is the right timing critical to communicate with stakeholders?

How

- How are they impacted by the change we are producing?
- How will the communications be delivered (personally, phone, video conference, meetings, etc.) to stakeholders?
- How much influence do they yield over the success of the information management effort?

Why

- Why does the stakeholder have to be involved (Role)?
- Why is stakeholder's relationship important?

Internal partner and support organizations are also stakeholders. They will provide support during and after the project and need to be set up for success. Though a joint responsibility, there are certainly responsibilities of the IM team in meeting their requirements and communicating what is needed in order for the project to be a long-term production success.

After listing out all the stakeholder parties, plans should be developed to manage the stakeholders of the project—not as an afterthought, but as a primary focus of the IM project. When you do this, you will find that you do not have the 5 stakeholders you thought you did, but you actually have 100.

To change the process for a New Product Introduction (utilizing Master Data Management) in one company, we listed 231 stakeholders. It's not just the people whose jobs are directly impacted. It's everyone who *cares* about the process changes. The Human Resources Manager needed to know about it to communicate it to prospective hires. Someone on the Legal team needed to know in order to understand if we were changing anything that would change how contracts are written (we were), frontline employees needed to be aware of the increased pace of product change, and Finance needed to approve any process changes that might affect cost.

Owners from the information management team should be assigned to the stakeholder management tasks based on existing relationships, personality and interest compatibility, bandwidth, and organizational and physical proximity.

●●●───

The process for Stakeholder Management is: List→Understand→Influence.

───

We nominally refer to the body of stakeholders on "our side" as Change Champions and expect them to carry the changes' messages throughout the organization.[2] A Change Champion should have influence and credibility within the organization. The Change Champion should possess knowledge and skills to help the development team secure commitment to change. The Change Champion can build organizational support for change.

There are many ways they can assist information management efforts. These include:
- Answering questions about business machinations in the development of the project
- Assisting in identifying key stakeholders' positions and how they may be influenced, by the Change Champions as well as by the information management team
- Weaving key messages into their formal and informal communications with their peers
- Contributing to Post-Implementation Job Roles (discussed next)
- Identifying post-implementation challenges and helping prepare the organization for them
- Ensuring testing is in alignment with core process changes

These Change Champions can dramatically increase the odds of a successful project through their influence and guidance.

───

[2] Stakeholders who have the most to lose because of change will be opponents to change.

Post-Implementation Job Roles Specifies How Jobs Will be Changed

If job roles are expected to change, we do not want to leave the official descriptions of the jobs out there in their former state. Doing so would leave an anchor for the affected stakeholders to the old way and it would also confuse any new people to those positions.

In many companies, there are official locations for job roles. These locations may include human resource descriptions and the files of the management of the positions affected. The Post-Implementation Job Roles task also aligns job performance and bonus metrics of the stakeholders to the project goals.

In most cases, this will be a progressive additive to the worker's roles and job descriptions. New organizational alignment and coordination responsibilities are also part of defining Post-Implementation Job Roles. The bottom line goal is to assure the right people are equipped to execute new processes and function with the new information management components at the right time.

Sales quotas, data entry volume, data entry quality, responsiveness to the new system, time to market, etc. metrics could change as a result of the new system. For a New Product Introduction system, sales quotas were planned to be increased slowly over time (as a result of increased capabilities) and job descriptions for many who worked in the product group were changed to reflect using the new system for bringing in new products.

Job Role Changes
- Examine job roles and titles to ensure that they best represent the work activities for each job role
- Job roles should have a clear purpose and area of responsibility within the process
- Review each process and identify what work activities belong in a job role and where there should be a hand off to another job role

Organizational alignment begins well before project close and the formal development of the new roles. Demonstrating how all the OCM work products work together during the project, the change managers will identify skills lacking in current functions and those who fill them. This is input into the OCM training work product, described next.

Training Development and Delivery Transfers the Knowledge Required

Those changing roles! We build IM projects and hope for change. However, doing so without Stakeholder Analysis and Post-Implementation Job Roles is just having blind hope. Similarly, stakeholders must be trained for their new roles. If you see a pattern here of project team responsibility, you are getting it! Too often, IM project team responsibilities seem to stop with the technical, implementation tasks. Keep in mind, I am not suggesting the project teams need to *execute* all of the Organizational Change Management tasks, but they do need to make sure they are completed. Ultimately, whether "outsourced" or not, the IM team has major responsibility for these tasks.

Training begins with a comprehensive needs assessment, which includes an assessment of current versus needed skills by the organization. Business process changes become the backdrop for the training. It allows the training to be role-based, helping participants know what needs to be done so they can be effective with the changes.

Training Development and Delivery could involve any number of mediums, modules, and events. Training could be informal, as in desk-side coaching of a single person, or it could be very formal, as in running multiple classes or webinars for hundreds of suppliers who will now use MDM for entering their supplies for the company. Training could involve the build of materials specific to end-use of the IM project. Pick the medium based on the training need and the best learning method for the stakeholder. Regardless, Training Development and Delivery is a very important Change Management task that conveys the specific expectations of the project to the affected stakeholders.

Training is an opportunity to grow the effectiveness and the careers of the participants, which is one of the biggest rewards of doing an IM project.

Answering the following questions can help piece together the content of the training:

1. Business Processes – What are the processes that are changing? What is new about them? What roles in the processes are changing?
2. Roles – What training is required to perform the new roles? What is the most effective training to get them there? How will the alternative training approaches be mapped to the participants?

For the more formal and multiperson at a time types of training, such as classes and webinars, logistics become a major component of the training development. Training registration, environment reservations and setup, reminders and post-training support infrastructure, are some of the items to master.

My personal favorite is a live webinar that is also recorded for posterity and for those who missed the live event. You may want to run the live webinar multiple times to be sure to accommodate everyone. If everyone is worldwide, this may include some late evenings or early mornings for the trainers. It is almost assured that multiple forms of training are going to be required. See Figure 17.1.

Deployment Preparation Ensures the Organization is Ready to Manage the Implementation

In the days prior to implementation, it is easy to get caught up in final changes from user acceptance testing, end-to-end testing, or whatever testing phase the development is going through at the time. However, anything about to go to production and start involving support teams and changing hands needs conscious attention to that aspect of the project.

Usually, the machines are supported by a production team, which may or may not ask all the right questions of the project team for the turnover.

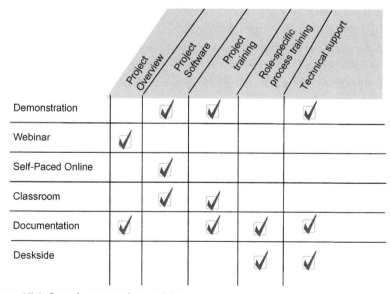

Figure 17.1 Sample approach to training.

The project team should be prepared with specific documentation related to how it expects production to be handled and how it expects to stay involved with the project post-production. This should be a final step in what has been an ongoing relationship with the production team.

What is the escalation for production failures in the middle of the night? Who will manage hardware and software patching? Who will make the call/expend the budget for additional disk/CPU/memory as the implementation grows? Who approves new users? Who resets passwords? What are the escalation procedures? What are the help desk procedures?

None of these are questions that you want to address at the moment of failure.

Communications Planning Ensures Continual Communication With the Affected Parties

The training may occur in anticipation of a go-live date, which, as we all know, is subject to change. Stakeholders become affected and job roles change on the go-live date. So, communicating the last, official go-live is essential.

Also, generally announcing the project at this time could begin the process of revision and improvement as it brings out new users who didn't participate in the project because they thought it wouldn't make it! General announcements also give weight to the importance of the project and provide a morale boost to the development team, who can see the organization is receiving the fruits of their labor.

This organizational awareness should be distributed in preestablished channels such as company newsletters, intranet sites, and general announcements. All of this needs to be set up beforehand or these communications will undoubtedly be late and less effective.

How about putting up a group picture of the team in the corporate lobby congratulating the success with some text talking about the project? Do something novel. Have fun with it.

ORGANIZATION CHANGE MANAGEMENT IS ESSENTIAL TO PROJECT SUCCESS

So, now you have identified and influenced stakeholders, officially set up new job roles, prepared for deployment, and delivered training and communications. Readiness to change applies to all the individuals implicated in these discrete components but it also applies to the organization as a whole. It's about culture. Culture eats strategy for lunch. OCM works the culture issues to the favor of the information management project.

It would be hard to argue against the criticality of any of these OCM work products, yet many do so tacitly by avoiding and ignoring them. Don't let solutions to these "soft" problems be "soft." Make them real, tangible, and part of an action–oriented framework. The tasks reviewed here identify and address major risks to IM projects early in the projects and provide an actionable framework for success.

Corporate Implications of a Focus on IM

The focus on Information Management has broader implications as well, which could be reinforced with OCM. They are:

1. The leadership/management team is reacting to its business environment.
2. Leadership/management strategizes approaches that impact its business environment.
3. Leadership/management fund initiatives that will change the internal environment to respond to the external business' environment.
4. Initiatives encompass projects that are targeted to change the business' products, services, and behaviors that affect people, processes, organizations, information, technology, policies, practices, procedures, etc.
5. Information management is an enabling component for the long-term "sustainability" and "survival" of organizations in the 21st Century.
6. To disregard the importance of Information Management and classify it as only a "cost without benefit" will severely inhibit future integrations.
   a. Technology changes will affect computing storage, speed/power, and communications. *These are only means for doing business.*
   b. Migrations/transitions will be required to update those technologies.
   c. Data (*which is the means that organizations use for decision making*) requires IM ensuring:
      i. Definition – Clarity, Uniqueness, Acceptability
      ii. Accuracy – Capture, Content, Format
      iii. Timeliness – Time-based Capture, Presentation
      iv. Relevance – Comprehension and usefulness in business context
7. So, a comprehensive IM approach is required of the leadership team to make enterprise-scope use of data, "big data," future predictive real-time analytics, database management systems opportunities, virtualization, and mobile delivery of high-quality data and information.

Information Management needs to be a managerial initiative that will be the basis for sustainable winners in the competitive worldwide market. Because IM is a philosophical and political position from an Organizational Change Management perspective, it really is the " Hard Stuff"! An information management program must have a focus beyond technology and address the people-related risks. Success will come from taking care of Organizational Change Management.

ACTION PLAN

- By project, choose the applicable OCM work products – don't skimp
- Assess all ongoing information management projects for their inclusion of OCM tasks
- Leave cycles in project estimates for OCM activities
- Ensure new information management projects include OCM tasks
- For each project
    - Identify and influence stakeholders
    - Set up new job roles
    - Deliver training
    - Deliver communications
    - Prepare for deployment

INDEX

Printed and bound by CPI Group (UK) Ltd, Croydon, CR0 4YY

03/10/2024

01040426-0018